HONDA

THE UK STORY

HONDA
THE UK STORY

Eric Dymock

DOVE PUBLISHING

First published in Great Britain in 1995 by
DOVE PUBLISHING
Old Chapel House, Sutton Veny, Wiltshire BA12 7AY

Designed by Ruth Dymock with
Andrew Barron & Collis Clements Associates

British Library Cataloguing-in-Publication Data. A catalogue
record for this book is available from the British Library

ISBN 0 9518750 5 1

Colour separation by Fotographics Ltd,
London and Hong Kong

Made and printed in Great Britain by
Butler & Tanner Ltd, Frome

CONTENTS

THE FIRST HONDAS

Honda Tadakatsu (1548-1610) was feudal lord of the Honda, a family from Mikawa province in central Japan.
They were loyal followers of Tokugawa Ieyasu (1542-1614) first of the Tokugawa Shoguns, who won battles in which the Honda took part as samurai warriors. Tadakatsu's son Honda Tadamasa (1575-1631) fought alongside him and in recognition of his service, in 1617 was given the castle of Himeji.

A statue of Honda Tadakatsu outside Himeji depicts him with a Buddhist 'rosary', a helmet which traditionally carried huge wooden antlers, and his spear, wryly nicknamed the dragonfly slicer. His armour is in the Honda museum at Himeji.

'They used to say man lived only 50 years, but with command of speed he can extend his lifespan. Doctors are not the only ones contributing to longer life. We should stop talking about distance; we should talk about time.' – Soichiro Honda.

Like Rolls-Royce or Isotta-Fraschini, Honda might have had a double-barrelled name. Takeo Fujisawa meant as much to Soichiro Honda and Honda Motor as the Hon C S Rolls did to Henry Royce, or Cesare Isotta to Vincenzo Fraschini in the founding of Isotta-Fraschini. Some of the world's best cars were the products of twin souls, one an engineer, the other a merchant, perhaps, or an accountant. Daimler and Benz were engineers, Count Albert de Dion and Georges Bouton left lasting legacies, but sometimes the double-barrelling was merely expedient, like Armstrong and Siddeley or Austin and Healey, affiliations that were woven into the very fabric of the motor industry.

There never was a Honda-Fujisawa; the only term ever formally coupled with Honda was "motor" and, like the Bavarian Motor Works or Bentley Motors, Honda Motor was first and foremost a maker of motors, and that meant engines. Ferrari Automobili, Jaguar Cars, Ford Motor Company, these were car makers every one and engine makers of quality as well, but Honda's key activity was eternally motors. It created engines for motorcycles, cars, generators, lawn mowers, agricultural machinery, and boats. It became the biggest engine maker in the world – and the eighth biggest car maker, twice the size

Stub exhausts of Soichiro Honda's Curtiss OX-5-engined Honda Special (right). The 1910 design weighed 350lb and gave an unreliable 90bhp at 1,400rpm

SOICHIRO HONDA

Soichiro Honda was born in a remote village in central Japan, on November 17, 1906, the eldest of nine children of a blacksmith. His father, the enterprising Gihei Honda, fought in the Russo-Japanese war but when peace came he turned to repairing bicycles. Soichiro was fascinated by his father's workshop, and the threshing machine at the local rice refinery.

At the age of eight his imagination was fired by seeing a Model T Ford, and when he finished school he was determined to work with cars. He started as an apprentice at a Tokyo garage in the prosperous era between the end of the first world war and the disastrous Great Kanto earthquake of 1923, but although he was achieving his ambitions to work with machinery he disliked the harsh social conditions he met with in post-feudal Japan.

The earthquake destroyed the garage, and only Soichiro and a senior apprentice remained to rebuild the business under Yuzo Sakakibara who later encouraged him to build a racing car. Using an old aircraft engine, a Curtiss 8-litre V-8 with 100bhp at 1,400rpm, Soichiro built everything else himself, which included carving the wooden wheel spokes.

Sakakibara gave Soichiro responsibility for a branch of the firm in Hamamatsu Komyo, where he built more racers, for oval tracks with only left-hand bends, using an offset Ford engine. This anticipated a (later discredited) vogue in Indianapolis racing car design. He tried supercharging and dealt with the problems it brought by fitting extra cooling radiators, and making valve seats from special materials.

Soichiro Honda won a number of races but his career nearly ended in the All-Japan Speed Rally of 1936 near Tokyo. As he approached the finish he crashed into a car leaving the pits, pitching himself and his younger brother, acting as riding mechanic, into the road. Soichiro had injuries to his face that left permanent scars, dislocated his shoulder and broke his wrist. His brother escaped with lesser injuries.

By way of consolation, his 120kph (75mph) average speed remained a Japanese race record for nearly 20 years.

In 1937 he set up Tokai Seiki Heavy Industry to make piston rings, a scarce commodity much in demand by the military. Honda patented his ideas on die-casting, but his first efforts were not a success. He had to learn metallurgy before he was in a position to supply Toyota (which took 40 per cent of the firm's equity) and the Nakajima Aircraft company. Soichiro designed automatic machinery for making piston rings and supplied them throughout the war for aircraft and truck engines. He also set up machine tools for making aircraft propellers, in a factory bombed by the Americans and finally almost destroyed by an earthquake in January 1945.

Unlike many Japanese intellectuals, Honda took Japan's defeat philosophically. He knew that a period of uncertainty lay ahead so he sold the remainder of the business to Toyota, expecting it to be broken up by the Americans, and took a year off. Typically unorthodox, he spent the time making sake and partying, then in October 1945 he set up the Honda Technical Research Institute which two years later became the Honda Motor Company.

His "bata-bata" (roughly the Japanese for "phut-phut") was an immediate success, and was the foundation of Honda's fortunes.

Unlike many of his Japanese contemporaries, Soichiro Honda was an extrovert who wore colourful clothes. Nonconformity, he claimed, was essential to an artist or innovator.

He instructed his biographers to dwell on the positive aspects of his firm's labour relations, describing it as a meritocracy although his personal relationships could be stormy and he would berate poor performance or shoddy workmanship. A noisy tirade could be followed by a well-aimed spanner. Soichiro's appearance on the shop floor with a missile in his hand could be a signal to take cover, yet he would claim that the prosperity of his company relied on lofty ideals such as trust in youth and promoting creative people.

Soichiro personally tested new models until the age of 65 and did not groom his son to take his place. Like Ferry Porsche, he effectively barred his family from senior posts. He retired from the company presidency in 1973 and withdrew from its affairs. A company prospers, he said, when its former head turns up as infrequently as possible, and he was adamant that not only should his family be excluded from the succession, but that the presidency should be gained on the basis of merit. "No matter how outstanding a company founder might be, that is no guarantee that his son is equally capable. The corporate presidency must be handed on to a person possessing the most distinguished qualities of leadership."

After he retired, he devoted himself to the Honda Foundation which aimed to harmonise technology with ecology, and served as vice-president of both the Tokyo Chamber of Commerce and Industry and of the Japanese Automobile Manufacturers' Association.

Soichiro Honda married in 1935 and died in August 1991 leaving a wife, Sachi, one son, and two daughters.

Soichiro Honda
(far left)

and with Takeo
Fujisawa
(below left)

Exposed valve
gear of the
8-litre V-8
Curtiss aero
engine in the
1920s Honda
Special (right)

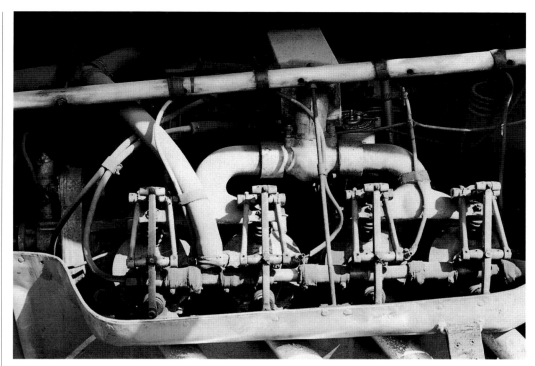

of BMW and Rover combined – turning out 8 million engines
of all kinds every year.

Honda Motor's roots went back to the 1930s with Soichiro
Honda's Tokai Seiki Heavy Industry desperately trying to
manufacture die-cast piston rings. They were brittle and they
broke, so Soichiro took night classes in metallurgy to get them
right. Later his little firm struggled for survival among the ruins
of post-war Japan, and only thrived as the economy recovered.
It became the world's largest manufacturer of motorcycles – by
1988 Honda had made 50 million of them and had nearly
350,000 on British roads in the 1990s – yet it was plainly at its
best with engines. Honda engines established their reputation
in motorcycles where precise detailing, good finish, and fine
balance were crucial. Honda went on to cars in the 1960s,
where partnerships of accomplished engineers and shrewd
merchants had a good track record. Honda – the company and
the man, along with Fujisawa – would, in due course, establish
their own credentials on the race-circuits of the world while
generating a reputation second to none on the road.

After 1945, social upheaval and occupation transformed
Japan. The bulk of Tokyo's wooden houses had been razed
by fire-bombings, the cities of Hiroshima and Nagasaki were
atomic wastelands. There were years of deprivation and
shortages to come after nearly 3 million were killed or seriously
wounded in the war. There were 9 million people homeless,
together with 2 million destitute citizens repatriated from
former Imperial territories adding to the burden. Rice
production was halved, and a land that had supported 35 million
in the 1880s was called upon to sustain 72 million.
Notwithstanding the efforts of the occupying forces there was
hunger, and a black market. Women gained the vote, land

THE FINEST BRIDGE, THE NIPPON-BASHI (BRIDGE),
AND ITS NEIGHBOOR-HOOD, DAIREN.

近附の其ゝ橋本日連大、比無麗壮 （連／大）

TAKEO FUJISAWA

Hideshiro Fujisawa's advertising agency kept his son Takeo in financial security until the Great Kanto earthquake which also affected Soichiro Honda. The fires that followed on 1 September, 1923, destroyed greater Tokyo, killing 140,000 people. Fujisawa lost everything and Takeo spent his schooldays in poverty.

The Wall Street Crash of 1929 and its repercussions on the economy led to a job shortage and Fujisawa joined the Imperial Army. His father found the cash to buy him out and in 1934 he found a job with a steel stockholding firm. Following the military takeover in Japan and the outbreak of the Sino-Japanese war, the steel firm's owner was called up for military service and 27-year-old Takeo Fujisawa found himself in charge.

His business skills flourished, but by 1945 Tokyo was once more devastated by firestorms raised by American bombing. Fujisawa moved out, and when the war ended he found the city destitute and in ruins. It was 1948 before he went back.

Soichiro Honda was 42 and looking for a backer, Fujisawa 38. Honda recalled the partnership: "If both Fujisawa and I had the same goal, say, like reaching the top of Mount Fuji, I would take one route while he took another because he had a different philosophy and personality. If we had taken the same route we might both have been finished off by a storm. We were able to communicate with each other because we were taking different courses. Fujisawa would say to me, 'I see trouble ahead, so be careful'. We had heart to heart communication although we were at different places and acted differently. Yet we had the same mountain to climb."

Fujisawa saw to cash flow. Once the motorcycles were a success he made dealers pay in advance and distributors' guarantee-money was a substantial source of Honda's 1950s investments in new plant and machinery. Of Soichiro he said: "If he had started talking about how much profit we would make next year I would have been disappointed. Such talk would imply concern about his personal income. He was a great person playing a leading role, so those of us who played supporting roles had to build a great theatre – a corporation – that would suit the leading actor."

It was astute Fujisawa who saw marketing opportunities in the 1950s before everyone else. Japan had 400 motorcycle dealers, but 55,000 bicycle retailers and he signed them up to sell the F-type Cub – with a bicycle engine – opening up a new working-class market and setting up different dealers for specialist models.

Fujisawa wanted Honda Motor to have experts in every field. He despised any system under which superiors evaluated juniors, because one indifferent superior could impede the progress of any number of juniors.

He retired on the 25th anniversary of Honda Motor's foundation, in September 1973.

reform and democracy changed the pattern of society, and Japan's adaptable culture embraced Western, particularly American, ways but life was a matter of harsh realities, getting on with things, making-do, improvising as never before.

The recovery was tackled with great vigour. There was a new spirit of enterprise, and individuals became citizens under the new regime rather than subjects as they had been under the old. In October 1946, after taking a year off, Soichiro Honda established the Honda Gijutsu Kenkyujo (Technical Research Institute). Like Tokai Seiki Heavy Industry, it was a grand title for a small factory in Hamamatsu on the south coast of Japan's main island, Honshu. The bulk of Mount Fuji lay to the north on the road to Tokyo. Soichiro liked ambitious-sounding names. He toyed with the idea of making textile machinery to meet the clothing shortage, but in the end he went back to his father's basic business — bicycles. Instead of repairing them, however, he fitted 500 of them with military surplus engines.

Japan at the dawn of the motor age. Bicycles, rickshaws and a tram on the Nippon-Bashi bridge (above left)

Hamamatsu branch of Art Shokai, Soichiro Honda's first management responsibility (above right)

1952 Model F two-stroke engine fixed on a bicycle (right). Honda made 7,000 a month

It was a practical contribution to Japan's predicament. The engines were small, primitive, inefficient Tohatsu two-strokes that had been used as generators for field communication equipment, and the motorised bikes were a boon in a country where buses and railways were unreliable and overcrowded, and cars next to useless thanks to the petrol shortage. The makeshift motorcycles were an immediate success. Honest peasants and black marketeers alike made their way to Honda with cash in hand. In the early days Honda's workers were making one of the machines each working day but they soon became faster at it.

The original stock of engines was quickly exhausted, so Soichiro's father sold some woodland for cash to develop a replacement. Work began on a 50cc two-stroke along the lines of the old generator engine with magneto ignition and a slide carburettor. Known as the A-type, it was mounted on a bicycle crossbar and drove the rear wheel via a belt with a primitive guard to keep it off the rider's leg. Honda provided the fuel as well, and, recalling that pine resin had been used (not very successfully) to meet the scarcity of aviation fuel during the war, bought a small pine forest and squeezed resin from the tree roots to mix with black-market petrol. The turpentine fuel sometimes took a lot of pedalling to light up, but the smoke and smell were essential to persuade the authorities that it was not rationed and conserved (and black-marketed) petrol. The smoky exhaust earned it an unsurprising nickname, The Chimney, ironic for a company that was to become a world leader in the technology of exhaust emission control.

First Honda engine (top right). Derived from war surplus generator engines, the two-stroke Model A was crude, slow, belt-driven and turpentine-fuelled. It sold well in post-war Japan

First real motorcycle, the Model D of 1949 (bottom right). Hand-made by Soichiro Honda and employees, it was called Dream because it fulfilled theirs

Once again the product was a success although commercially problematical. There were no Honda dealers, little mercantile framework, and banking and credit systems were in disarray. The business had to be properly organised and in September 1948, with capital of 1 million yen (then about £1,000), was set up as the Honda Motor Company. The B-type motorcycle was launched with a 90cc engine and Japan's first post-war delivery drivers were offered a tricycle version with an open-topped box on the back, vertically-sprung girder forks, and, by way of acknowledgment that Hondas were now fully-equipped practical road machines, a solitary headlamp.

Alas, single-minded engineering was not enough, and a commercial overhaul was needed to ensure a realistic cash flow and proper accounting. Takeo Fujisawa joined as managing director, the firm's capital was increased and the D-type two-stroke 98cc Dream, with a bicycle-style saddle, telescopic forks, and rigid unsprung rear wheel, came out in August 1949. The triangular frame was heavy and the engine produced a bare 3bhp, yet Fujisawa took the opportunity to knock the retail trade into shape and make it aware of the new commercial realities. The D-type had some unfortunate shortcomings. Honda's competitors had tubular frames that looked better than the D-type's rough pressed-steel structure, and mudguards

Japan back on its wheels (above). Post-war reconstruction was propelled by demand for transport. Honda was one of dozens of small manufacturers who put engines on anything that would move that did not get clogged with mud on Japan's rough war-torn unmade roads. Fujisawa told Honda he needed to design something better.

The way to achieve technical superiority over rivals' buzzing two-strokes was with a relatively sophisticated four-stroke, the Dream E-Type, which set new standards and achieved new production records. It also broke speed records at a dizzy 45mph (72kph) in pre-production tests and 130 were made every day in a new Tokyo factory. Competition was keen; in 1950 Japan had 200 motorcycle manufacturers, with names like Fuji, Pointer, Showa, Sanyo, and Rocket, each producing a handful of machines. Tohatsu was the biggest, making 70,000 bikes in 1955, twice as many as Honda which was sent a disbelieving Ministry of Trade and Industry official to check its figures, suspicious they were invented to boost the factory's petrol allocation.

The E-type overwhelmed the opposition. All but four rivals went out of business – Bridgestone being the last, in 1968 – and Honda reached a technical milestone with the four-stroke power unit that provided it with supremacy in engine design and construction for years to come. Not only was the E-type a sophisticated four-stroke in a market awash with two-strokes, but its 146cc single cylinder had three overhead valves – two inlet and one exhaust – worked by pushrods at the back of the cylinder from a camshaft on top of the crankcase. It was a level of technical superiority that some of its rivals failed to reach for many years and was indicative of Honda's most often-preferred solution to problems – advanced technology.

KIYOSHI KAWASHIMA
In March 1947 Soichiro Honda interviewed a graduate from the Hamamatsu college of technology. Kiyoshi Kawashima wanted to design high-performance engines and his enthusiasm for speed took Honda's fancy. In 1951 Kawashima designed Honda's crucial E-type 146cc overhead valve four-stroke which was 10 years ahead of its competitors. He not only laid down the theory and drew it up, but he also tested the prototype in July 1951, beating Honda and Fujisawa from Hamamatsu to the top of the nearby Hakone mountain.

In 1973 Kawashima was promoted from president of research and development to president of Honda Motor Company, signing the Rover agreement in 1979 and retiring to the post of supreme adviser in 1983.

Competing motorcycles in post war Japan included a general purpose Mazda tricycle (right) and the Rabbit (below right) in a retrospective display at the Tokyo motor show

The Korean war that began in 1950 brought changes in Japan's circumstances inconceivable in the aftermath of the second world war. It hastened Japan's return to the international community and revitalised the economy. The resulting commercial prosperity brought a stable exchange rate, relaxed government controls on business and initiated a privatisation programme. The economy grew and though there were penalties for success – such as labour unrest throughout Japanese industry not wholly resolved until 1954, and a recession following the war – progress edged forward through the 1950s. At the same time Honda was feeling the effects of competition spurred on by the healthier economy.

The market was becoming choosy and the Cub, an asthmatic clip-on bicycle engine of which Honda made 6,500 a month, fell from favour. The new 90cc J-type Benly motorcycle was also failing because its engine was noisy. The Juno scooter's plastic body was making its engine overheat. Eventually the workforce and management had to sit down with suppliers who were owed money and the Mitsubishi Bank to work out how to curtail production until things were put right.

The 125cc Benly JB and the Dream SA (250cc) and SB (350cc) proved to be the answer. They took Honda to the head of Japanese motorcycle production in 1955 and, more importantly for its long term prospects, Soichiro Honda was able to revive his obsession with motor sport. In March 1954 a Honda team took part in a race in Sao Paulo, Brazil, and Soichiro committed them to entering the TT races in Britain. In June he made an exploratory visit to the Isle of Man. In 1955 Hondas won the 350cc and 500cc classes and manufacturers' team prize in the first Mount Asami all-Japan motorcycle endurance race. But already the stage was set for a wider range of activities.

"The dream of my youth was to build an automobile with my own hands and have it dominate world motor racing competition," Soichiro said in 1954, when employee and national morale was low. "I am committed to have Honda Motor tackle this formidable task to illustrate our capabilities

The TT world Honda joined (below). Racing on the Isle of Man had its own atmosphere and tradition. Spectators at Ginger Hall enjoyed an intimate view in 1957, three years after Soichiro Honda's first visit

and set a standard for Japanese industry."

Honda had a number of reasons for embracing motor sport besides simply courting publicity to encourage sales. Morale at the plants in Japan was not high. The hiatus over the Benly had only just been solved and following the success of the E-type Dream more than 2,000 new workers were taken on. Their sudden arrival brought unrest, there were protests over Soichiro's abrasive style of management, and even sabotage. Soichiro recalled, "Most of the workers were young and quite attracted to the idea of winning races, particularly because we had just lost the war. The thought of hoisting the Japanese flag on the Isle of Man seemed very tempting." Fujisawa likewise supported the entry to motorcycle racing. "I'll solve the problem of money. You work on winning races," he told Soichiro.

Honda's first win in Europe (top right). Jim Redman and Bob McIntyre (with helmet) and a 250cc Honda four at Aintree in 1960

Ultra-lightweight (bottom right). The 50cc twin-cam screamers introduced for the 1962 TT averaged 70mph on the Mountain circuit, revving to 10,000rpm. Here shown without the fairing. East German defector Ernst Degner won for Suzuki, with Honda second and third

To his great dismay, Soichiro found that the NSUs and Gileras racing in the Isle of Man were producing three times the power of his best Hondas. Their tyres and chains were superior and he began to worry about his chances of beating them. He had long admired NSU, and when the Honda C70 road bike appeared in 1957 it owed something to NSU inspiration. Even so, the special version of the E-type Dream was still only revving to 7,000rpm while the revered opposition was reaching 10,000rpm. Tadashi Kume and Kimio Shimmura, given the job of designing the racing engines, were young, keen and innovative, but they faced a daunting task.

"We were told to start designing racing engines right after joining the company," Kume recalled. "Nothing could have been more interesting and we were very excited. No other company would have provided us with such a challenge." Once the design was completed the new engines were assembled by Kiyoshi Kawashima, head of the design section, the competitive spirit spilling over from racing to provide a hothouse atmosphere forcing new ideas out of young designers and preparing them for senior positions later on. Kume followed Kawashima as president of Honda.

Soichiro's contribution to the process was crucial. The new engine's connecting rods broke under test and, although making them heavier and stronger seemed an obvious solution, he invoked an old Japanese proverb about large trees blowing over in strong winds while slender bamboo only bent, and made them smaller and lighter instead. He also initiated research on timing chains that would withstand high speeds and the violent thrust reversals encountered in racing.

"Two years after we declared our intention of taking part in the Isle of Man races, as the technical levels of components and mechanical features of the engines improved, we were able to come up with one powerful enough to compete with foreign motorcycles," Soichiro recalled. "The young engineers did a good job, but that was not enough to assure us of victory in the TT. The rider is as important as the machine. Even if we had the same level of performance as our competitors, we still could not win without a top rider. We needed to develop a racing machine that would win even without a superior rider so that when we had one, victory would be certain."

Soichiro knew that the key to power lay in a close study of combustion, and new ways of exploring what went on inside the cylinder were put in hand. Changes in design were slow to come about and in the second Mount Asami race Honda won only the 350cc class, Soichiro complaining a little sourly that the overall winners had imitated foreign technology. "We must win the Isle of Man Tourist Trophy through our own technology no matter how hard it is to develop," he said.

The reputation of the TT races in the 1950s was high. What Wimbledon was to tennis, the World Cup to football, or the Olympics to athletics, the TT was to motorcycling. Safety campaigners worried about the deaths and injuries to riders, but to a society still recovering from world war, almost anything

Honda won the 500cc motocross championship in 1979 with Graham Noyce. Belgian André Nalherbe won in 1981 and 1982, followed by fellow-countrymen Georges Jobé and Eric Geboers (far left), in 1987 and 1988. Dave Thorpe won in 1985, 1986, and 1989

With sump guard and aluminium frame, the Africa Twin celebrates Paris-Dakar Rally (above)

CBR 600F, top-selling sports roadster in the 1990s (left)

Mike Hailwood scrapes his foot on the Sachsenring track during East German 500cc Grand Prix (below), worries at the Belgian Grand Prix in 1967 (right), and on his last ride on a works Honda 500 in Italy the following year (far right)

MIKE HAILWOOD
Stanley Michael Bailey Hailwood MBE, GM, accomplished Honda's first TT victories in 1961 when he became the first rider to win three TTs in a single week, – one of which was on a Norton. He won the Senior and Lightweight 250cc in 1966 and made a clean sweep of Senior, Junior, and Lightweight again the following year. Hailwood's score of 14 TTs and 10 world championships were the foundation for his reputation as the greatest motorcycle racer of his time, perhaps the greatest ever.

Hailwood was a racer's racer, the epitome of glamour and success who turned in a winning performance every time he rode. He set the standards by which other riders judged themselves, and on a competitive machine he was in a class of his own. His 1967 108.77mph record for the 37.75 mile Isle of Man course on a 500cc four-cylinder Honda was not broken until 1975.

Hailwood found the Honda difficult to ride after the MV Agusta he had been used to, and Honda's solution of making the engine more powerful only made matters worse. The problem lay in its handling and Hailwood came to share the view of John Surtees, for whom he later drove cars, that a similar philosophy persisted when Honda went into Formula One motor racing.

In 1978 Hailwood delighted his fans with a brilliant comeback to TT racing after 11 years. At the age of 38 he astounded newer and younger stars with his apparently fearless mastery of the motorcycle.

His reputation for raw courage was never better deserved than in 1974 when he stepped into the flames of Clay Regazzoni's burning BRM at Kyalami, South Africa, and calmly pulled him out. It was a brave and selfless act which saved Regazzoni's life and earned Hailwood the George Medal for gallantry.

Hailwood's riding talent did not depend wholly on valour. Born into a wealthy Oxford motorcycling family, he left school and went straight into his father's motorcycle business with no mechanical training. He joined Triumph as an apprentice but was soon riding competitively and, before long, professionally.

Hailwood said: "I don't think it is necessary to live like a candidate for a monastery," a reference to rivals' abstemiousness when racing, a habit he never caught.

His decision to go into car racing was prompted by the Honda motorcycle works team's withdrawal at the end of 1967. He was asked to go to Japan and instead of signing a contract for 1968 was invited to talk to the directors. "I sat there hoping they would make it short and I could go and sample the nightlife, when I realised the conversation was not going as I expected. Instead of contracts I was getting the 'regret' routine. You know, the 'regret that we ...'

and 'regretfully' which added up to Honda pulling the chain on their bike ambitions and as they put it, giving me the opportunity to look elsewhere. It was a bit late for that so I retired and went in for motor racing instead." Honda paid off his 1968 contract and gave him a couple of racing bikes for international races so that his services would be denied to rival makers. "I was also a bit peeved at losing a world championship for the second time through no fault of my own."

He raced John Wyer Gulf GT40s in long-distance events with some success but in single-seaters never attained the heights that he had on two wheels, although he did win the European Formula Two championship in 1972. He was a notably safe and skilled competitor and certainly among the fastest but, apart from one second and two fourth places, his grand prix score was modest. He broke his legs badly in a Yardley McLaren at the Nürburgring in 1974 and that effectively ended his grand prix career. But his heart was never far from motorcycles and he kept his TT-winning 500/4 of 1966 and 1967 in his rambling house at Holyport, Berkshire. He used to tell foreign inquirers that **MBE** stood for Motor Bike Engineer.

"Mike the Bike" Hailwood died with his young daughter in a road accident in 1981, leaving car and bike enthusiasts alike stunned and saddened.

undertaken voluntarily seemed relatively safe after the perils thrust on it between 1939 and 1945. Courage was a key ingredient for a motorcycle racer, as important as technical or tactical skill, and enthusiasts followed the fortunes of the annual event in detail. The prestige of the British motorcycle industry hung on the TT, and the classic makes of Norton, AJS, BSA, and Velocette were already under pressure from MV Agusta, Moto Guzzi, Gilera, Montesa, Mondial, Benelli, and NSU, which won the 250cc and 125cc races when Soichiro was there in 1954. The Isle of Man TT was still a picturesque event where Boy Scouts ran errands, the bulk of the entrants were amateur, and John Surtees could still collide with stray cows walking across the course in 1956.

It was the golden age of Geoff Duke and the Norton with its Featherbed frame, single-cylinder engine and crackling open exhaust, Les Graham on the "porcupine" AJS, 90mph lap speeds, Johnny Lockett, Artie Bell. Multi-cylinder machines with whining engines were still new and exciting, supplanting the hearty 500cc single cylinder "double-knocker". When Les Graham joined MV Agusta in 1951 his Senior TT bike had a shaft-drive and, like the Gilera, a dramatic transverse four-cylinder engine that changed the ideology of the sports motorcycle for ever.

Soichiro watched as the silver NSUs faced up to Moto Guzzi in the massed start of the Lightweight TT. The NSUs had streamlined shells with front mudguards pointed like duckbills and shallow windscreens. They streaked ahead from the beginning, their riders small, slim men finishing first (Werner Haas), second, third, fourth, and sixth. It was a similar story in the ultra-lightweight (125cc) race on the short Clypse course when Rupert Hollaus (NSU) beat the experienced Carlo Ubbiali (MV) after 10 laps of close competition. It was NSU's last year as a works team. The European motorcycle market was in decline, and the cost of racing was high. It not only cost cash, it also cost the lives of Hollaus and Haas, and NSU withdrew in 1955. In 1957 Moto Guzzi had a V-8, but AJS no longer entered a works team. Joe Craig, ex-rider and stubborn stalwart of Norton Motors, died in a car crash and Norton ended 33 years of racing in the TT. Bob McIntyre set the island's first 100mph lap before Gilera too retired its racing department along with DKW and Guzzi. Only MV, BMW, and Morini were left as European factory teams.

The two men who scored Honda's first major success in mainland Europe: Tom Phillis (left) and Jim Redman at Monza late in 1961

Supercub (top). Over three quarters of a million were built in the first full production year of 1958.

Ten years later, it was still good for helmetless, carefree riding.

CUB and SUPERCUB

Towards the end of the 1950s the Japanese market was overflowing with motorcycles. The industry was making around three-quarters of a million a year, its home market was well protected by tariff barriers so it had been able to charge profitable prices, but competition was growing keener, margins were falling and if it was going to expand it had to expand abroad.

Honda's answer was two new models, the first overhead camshaft twin, the 247cc C70, and the astonishing "step-thru" Super Cub that provided wheels for not only the teeming millions of the Pacific rim countries and south-east Asia, but the industrialised west as well. American Honda was established with the advertising slogan, "You meet the nicest people on a Honda".

The Super Cub was a stroke of genius. Honda rarely made anything the cheapest on the market, and although the Super Cub was inexpensive it was well-constructed with a 50cc four-stroke engine, a single air-cooled cylinder facing forwards into the airstream, pressed steel frame, swinging-arm rear suspension and a forward-link spring at the front. It had deep

mudguards and, for a small scooter, big wheels so that it could be used on dirt roads. By 1983 it sold 15 million, in the 1990s it reached 20 million and continued to sell almost unchanged with 50cc, 75cc, or 90cc engines.

The first 50cc Super Cub had 4.5bhp when it came out in August 1958, thanks to Honda's new awareness of combustion techniques and securing reliable power from small cylinders. It had a lively turn of speed, electric starter, and a centrifugal clutch making it easy to ride and handled well. The "step-thru" design made it attractive to inexperienced riders and its astonishing economy made it attractive to everybody.

Monkey bike,
the CZ, had
a 50cc engine
(top right)

Would it fit
in boot of
a 1956-1962
Ford Zodiac II?
(bottom right)·

By the time Honda came to the line in 1959, motorcycle racing had changed out of all recognition. It was entering a new phase and students of design could see what Honda had learned, especially from NSU, and the RC142 borrowed suspension and other features from the 1954 NSU twins even though its backbone frame was already out of date. It was soon replaced by a double-loop Norton- or Gilera-style of frame which improved the handling. Honda's engines developed 16bhp at 14,000rpm, and they won the manufacturers' team prize, and finished 6th, 7th, and 8th in the 125cc event. In 1960 Honda entered again and finished 4th, 5th, and 6th in the 250cc class, and 6th, 7th, 8th, 9th, and 10th in the 125cc. Like Porsche at Le Mans, Honda gained respect and admiration for reliability in the TT long before it gained a single outright win.

This came in 1961 when Honda took the first five places in both the 250cc and 125cc races. The *Daily Mirror* said the machines were, "built like fine watches", and Soichiro Honda declared: "Only by winning in the Isle of Man can we become a world enterprise selling our products internationally." The Australian rider Tom Phillis won the 125cc world championship, helping Honda towards the global goal for which Soichiro yearned.

The 1961 winner in both cases was arguably the greatest motorcycle racer of all time, Mike Hailwood. Honda's early efforts at the TT with Japanese riders, despite Soichiro's rhetoric, were worthy but ultimately unsuccessful. "We paid foreign riders five or six million yen each, which was a lot of money," Soichiro said. "When we entered the Formula One grand prix motor races we paid foreign drivers 10 times as much. Good riders were eager to win. They made demands, they told us when the machine wobbled or the brakes were not good enough, which raised our technical standards. Japanese racers were not like that. They didn't tell us anything." The following year Jim Redman (250cc and 350cc) and Luigi Taveri (125cc) won world championships, tightening Honda's grip on small-capacity racing.

Road-going motorcycles crucial to Honda's development included the C70, the first-generation 250cc twin with a four-speed gearbox in unit with the engine, the cylinders leaning forwards, pistons running together, and a single overhead camshaft. The frame and forks were heavy-looking steel pressings with messy welds, the mudguards large and the brakes small. Yet the C70 had a mirror and indicators, the C71 an electric starter, the CS71 a dual seat, and the RC70 was a sensual off-road variant with open exhausts running up the side of the machine. The C90 was the same bike reduced to 125cc . and the CB90, a sports version. The pressed-steel frame gave way to a stiff tubular one, the brakes were changed to a twin-leading shoe design, the styling was improved and so was the handling. Honda it seemed could learn fast and incorporate lessons from racing into its street bikes, something that British makers had failed to do for generations. The Honda small twins scarcely qualified to join the pantheon of motorcycling classics,

The ST50 or DAX flowered seat (left, top) lent a fragrant air to the step-thru engine (left, bottom) with forward-facing finned cylinder and 50cc or (here) 70cc

yet they were among the most popular, practical, and deeply loved motorcycles of their time.

It was an astonishing accomplishment, for motorcycling was still primarily a means of transport in Europe, not a leisure activity. Motorcycles were still used for going to work and making social journeys; the motorcycle was still thought of in the same way as a family friend or familiar furniture. Change was not undertaken lightly, the motorcycling crowd were very traditional, set in their ways, knew what they liked, and distrusted gadgets. There were still plenty of old bikes running in the 1950s with girder forks, and family sidecars were by no means uncommon.

The Honda Super Cub was to motorcycles what the Model-T Ford and the Volkswagen Beetle were to cars. Of Honda's first 50 million motorcycles, 17 million were Cub "step-thru" commuter bikes of 50cc, 70cc, and 90cc, made from 1958 on, which had pressed-steel frames and leading axle forks with primitive springs. Fujisawa, master of marketing, coaxed Soichiro to introduce it following a trip to Europe in 1956 during which they searched West German showrooms looking for a gap in the market between the Lambretta and the full-blown motorcycle. A year later when a mock-up Cub was made, Fujisawa, in his enthusiasm, resolved to set up a new factory at Suzuka to make 30,000 a month. It was a bold move. Honda's best seller was managing no better than 2,000 to 3,000 a month, yet Fujisawa planned the biggest motorcycle factory in the world to make 10 times as many.

Honda's next masterstroke was the Benly C92 of 1959 with a 125cc high-revving four-stroke twin-cylinder engine, introduced to a British market accustomed to BSA Bantams, James Captains and Francis-Barnetts with Villiers two-stroke engines that dated back in many respects to the 1930s. Almost the only concession 1950s British bikes made to modern

Teenage delight, the 1967 SS50 (far right)

Racy upswept exhausts on the 50cc and 90cc line at Suzuka factory (below)

motorcycling was telescopic forks and, sometimes, plunger rear suspension. Triumphs had faired-in headlamps, which were a bit Flash Harry, and real enthusiasts remained suspicious of Japanese motorcycles with high-revving aluminium engines instead of the familiar slow-turning plodders with cylinders made of good old solid cast-iron. The Japanese pressed-steel frames were despised because they looked like scooters, and leading-link forks were cheap-jack at best, downright dangerous at worst. Japanese bikes were scorned for their lack of pulling power, poor handling and, for all the customers knew, short lifespan.

Hondas did not leak oil, they did not need kick-starting and had well-finished overhead-cam engines that revved to 14,000 or 15,000rpm, lasted surprisingly well and delivered power smoothly and consistently. The bikes were equipped with accessories such as rev counters, dual seats, and flashing indicators. They were expensive but they were more reliable and better value than the British makes and Honda riders did not carry out running repairs.

There is not much doubt that Japanese imports hastened the end of the British motorcycle industry. A London Design

Classic Honda fours (above). Palmy days for a CB550F with sweeping exhausts (right) and a yellow-tanked CB750F

The shape of a superbike, the CB750 K4 of 1971 (left): with its air-cooled, 8-valve, single overhead cam, four cylinder engine, it could do 123mph. It had dry-sump lubrication, and disc brake at the front

Gleaming 4-carb engine (left, below)

Mick Woollett, sports editor of *Motor Cycle* tests a CB750 at Brands Hatch (below)

CB750

The motorcycle that secured Honda's future was the **CB750** of October 1968 with a stunning four-cylinder air-cooled overhead camshaft transverse engine, like the racing motorcycles of the day.

Honda technology was, as ever, engine-led, and although the 120mph **CB750** had handling that was less well thought out than the glorious unit providing power in gleaming abundance, its architecture was masterly. If anybody could take such care over an engine's external appearance, the argument ran, its internals must be even better. A powerful motorcycle became the smart way to get about crowded towns and the **CB750** filled the role perfectly.

Some of its other features were less agreeable. Routine servicing or adjustments had still to be carried out and some could be almost impossible for the amateur mechanic accustomed to cheap and cheerful British bikes. Many an enthusiast was dismayed to discover he could not work on the valve gear without taking the engine out.

For a while the 750 had little competition. It sold in 1969 for £680 against the **BSA Rocket 3**, the **Triumph Trident**, and the **Norton Commando** at around £620 at what turned out to be a watershed time. In 1970 it was "a connoisseur's dream", according to *Motorcycle Sport*, while a Trident 3 tested in the same issue refused to idle evenly, leaked oil, and was suspected of rusting. In contrast to the Honda's eye-catching instrument display, some of the Triumph's dials were not even lit at night. The sports fours that followed became Honda classics along with the mighty 24-valve double overhead cam six-cylinder **CBX** of 1978.

Museum exhibition in 1992 recalled its collapse in the brief decade between 1960 and 1970, leaving a market still worth over £200 million a year to imports. British motorcycles enjoyed leadership in the UK and elsewhere throughout the 1950s, but by the 1960s faced competition first in commuter bikes and mopeds, then throughout the two-wheeler market.

Soon only one motorcycle in 100 sold in Britain was locally made. Honda took 45 per cent of the market, Yamaha 23 per cent, and Kawasaki 7.8 per cent; by 1990, 95 per cent of all the motorcycles sold in Britain were Japanese, the remainder Italian or East European. Royal Enfield, Triumph, BSA, and Norton were gone. Enfield survived as a quirky Indian re-creation, Norton and Triumph struggled fitfully, but their great factories and world reputations were gone.

Design Magazine was clear about the cause: "Even the most patriotic British rider was seduced from the austere traditional path of virtue by lights that worked, electric starter motors and freedom from eyeball-buzzing vibration. Riders no longer thought it part of motorcycling's rich tapestry to sit by a wet roadside with their hands wrist-deep in an oily clutch."

Bert Hopwood put it more succinctly in his book, *Whatever Happened to the British Motorcycle Industry?* published by Heynes in 1981. Hopwood spent his life designing some of the best motorcycles made in Britain including Triumphs, BSAs, and the Norton Dominator. Notwithstanding his bitterness at being scorned by the old British motorcycle firms, he assigned responsibility for the disaster firmly to the managements and recalled the consternation created by the news that Honda was about to produce a 750cc machine. The Japanese had been regarded as good at making mopeds, but the idea of them competing on level terms scarcely crossed the minds of directors at Triumph and Norton and Associated Motorcycles. Advanced designs of new motorcycles were ready to appear, there was no lack of talent or expertise but the investment necessary to bring them out was never forthcoming. Money frittered away in racing, according to Hopwood, should have been spent on new models of which Honda now had plenty.

The Cub and the Benly ran from mid-1960 to 1965, the 250cc family was CB72, CB250, CB350, and CB360. The 750cc family included the CB500 which was effectively a smaller 750, and there was also the 450cc family. Hondas now had plenty of horsepower but the brakes were less than perfect and the Japanese proved tardy in bringing in disc brakes. Chassis development lagged behind engines. The suspension gave indifferent handling, and Japanese tyres remained firmly in the past, with no radials until the 1980s. Responses to complaints about the bikes' behaviour in the wet that they should be ridden only in the dry brought no comfort to those riding in the British climate. There was even a problem in racing when triangular section tyres and the 500/4 proved capable of frightening even Mike Hailwood.

The small four-cylinder road bikes were gems of high efficiency in a mediocre world, even though some were in

Turbocharged imbroglio. Uprated from 500, the CX650 (below) fulfilled the promise of the turbo with 100bhp at 8,000rpm. It did a thrilling 135mph

production a relatively short time owing to indifference in the United States where they were too sporty or in some cases too "European". The CB500 and 550/4 of 1974 were smaller versions of the triumphant CB750 with all the features that made the big machine such a success. The CB400/4 was more compact, with the same dramatic swirl of exhaust pipes curving down the front, and a uniform surge of speed that led Soichiro to declare it the smoothest Honda ever. It was well-conceived with good brakes, good handling, and a silky single-overhead-cam engine, though, with a top speed of around 104mph, not exceptionally fast.

Opposition to the big 750 was not long coming from Kawasaki, the world's fourth largest engineering company, with the 903cc Z1, which had double overhead cams and did 130mph. It was a challenge to Honda so far as the market was concerned, and Kawasaki's racing reputation thrived with a popular world champion, Barry Sheene.

Yamaha, too, came into contention and Honda's response in 1980-81 was a proliferation of new models that turned out to be little short of disastrous. At the time there were 900 UK

The incomparable Hailwood at the start of the 1967 Senior TT (far right), and clipping the apex of a corner in Ramsey (right) to win at 105.62mph – his nearest rival was 6mph slower. He won against Agostini's MV Agusta in the Junior

dealers – against 270 in the 1990s – selling nearly 90 road-going models and, although their popularity scarcely faltered, trying to cover every niche in the market was wasteful, and things began to go wrong.

High technology failed the CB500T when quality broke down. Changes to one version were not a success following problems with generator units, and routing cables through a hole in the handlebar upright so large that it weakened the structure was serious enough for a recall campaign.

Technology was being applied apparently for its own sake, and the CBX550 did little to put things right. The first VF750 of 1982, a V-4 with shaft drive, was heavy and handled badly, but a turning point was reached with the replacement VF750F. It was good where its predecessor was bad, did 140mph, and obtained rave reviews until a *Motorcycle News* strip-down test revealed serious wear on the camshafts and cam chain tensioners. It recovered in time, because Honda put its house back in order. Quality improved and the next major model, the CX500, was a 76 degree V-twin with shaft drive and water cooling that became a bestseller. Water-cooled engines were lighter, smaller, more compact, and their consistent running temperatures ensured they met emission-control standards. It was a bike that was popular with the demanding dispatch rider market for its thorough-going reliability even though its pushrod, lumpy, slow-revving engine seemed the very antithesis of everything high-revving Honda stood for.

The turbocharged CX650 exemplified Honda's aptitude for an engineering challenge. It was not much else because when the red-hot turbo was quenched with rainwater its housing tended to shatter. Its short career led to a segregation of Honda's engineering and marketing, and subsequently to the

Versatile and
compact;
a diesel tractor
with front
loader and
back-hoe
attachments
(below)

VFR750 V-4, perhaps the best complete road-going motorcycle of all time. Honda threw all its resources at it, and from a low starting point its reputation recovered.

The VFR750 became certain of success in Britain after Honda UK, finding it had nothing for its grand prix celebrity Ron Haslam to ride in the annual Easter Britain v America match race series, put him on a standard VFR750 against international stars on racing machines. In one rain-swept televised heat Haslam finished third, and within two days Honda UK's entire year's allocation of VFR750s was sold. It was not entirely equitable; Haslam was a brilliant match for the conditions and his mount less highly-strung than those of his opponents, but a road-going motorcycle that could keep up with real racers seemed too

TRACTORS
Power equipment not only demanded technical proficiency, it needed style. Honda learned from its motorcycle experience that a wide range of products created demand but it had to have an appearance that tempted customers. It achieved it in the way Colin Chapman gave Lotus style in the 1960s, by furnishing every component with a finish and demeanour that inspired its customers with confidence.

Lotus racing cars had well-finished castings, polished components where polish was not strictly necessary, gleaming paintwork where something less glossy might have been passed off as good enough.

Honda tractors were made with an elegance and form that matched the cars and the motorcycles on the principle that if the outside looked good, the inside probably looked good as well. Soichiro Honda's early lessons in metallurgy

gave all Honda products a singular shine, the aluminium die-castings had a precision that not only gave them a distinctive sheen, it enabled them to be assembled with an accuracy that made them oil-tight and businesslike to engineers and non-engineers alike. Cable runs were tidy, wiring was clipped with a precision that would not have looked out of place in an aircraft or a nuclear power plant and even humdrum tractors had technical dignity.

John Williams (No 18) and Bill Smith on 750s for the TT of 1976 (far left)

Gleaming chrome and bright die-cast aluminium shine in the evening light on a 16-valve water-cooled CB1000 Super Four

good to be true. The VFR750 was motorcycling's E-Type Jaguar, an affordable, docile, well-behaved, and beautiful machine with the handling and performance of a thoroughbred.

Back in 1967 Mike Hailwood had won the 250cc and 350cc world championships and Honda announced its withdrawal from motorcycle racing after he narrowly failed to win the 500cc title for which Honda waited until 1983. By then it had recovered from the four-stroke NR500's agonising return to grand prix road racing at Silverstone, won its first motocross world championship with Graham Noyce, and in 1986 finished first, second, third, fifth, and sixth in the rough, tough, and dangerous Paris-Dakar Rally. The 500cc title went to Freddie Spencer in 1983 and in 1985 he won both the 250cc and 500cc titles in a convincing triumph for Honda as it returned once again to the competitive, aggressive, and greatly altered world of Formula One grand prix motor racing which it had last been in during the gentle, distant 1960s.

Soichiro Honda passed on the leadership in 1973 to Kiyoshi Kawashima, then Tadashi Kume and, subsequently, Nobuhiko Kawamoto, all engineers still convinced, as Soichiro Honda had been, that motor sport not only gave Honda a good name but also motivated the engineers back home. Kawashima, a Honda veteran and designer of its first four-stroke engine, laid down the racing engines for the 1950s and 1960s TT races, and Kume was responsible for the engines with which Honda entered single-seater motor racing with Yoshio Nakamura - a long-time Honda employee who had been in charge of early car projects - as team manager in 1964.

The 1960s programme did not go altogether according to plan. Honda knew that making engines was what it was best at and wanted to put Kume's engines into a state-of-the-art chassis while working on cars of its own for later. Putting engines into somebody else's cars was the path to glory adopted by Coventry-Climax, which made power units for forklift trucks and fire-pumps. Ferrari farmed out engines from time to time and soon Repco, Cosworth, Maserati, and BRM would follow suit. Honda bought a Cooper to study, and approached Colin Chapman and Jack Brabham, and it looked as though a deal could be struck to put a new V-12 into a Lotus driven by Jim Clark. The combination of the world's best driver with a Honda engine in a purpose-built Lotus chassis would have been formidable. Chapman went to Japan to persuade Soichiro Honda that Lotus should have the Formula One engine and Brabham could make-do with Formula Two.

Brabham had earmarked the engine of the S1300 sports car - a sort of Honda Lotus Elite, never produced - that Kawamoto was working on as the basis for a smaller Formula Two engine on a visit to the research and development department in the 1960s. A 1-litre, 16-valve four-cylinder unit, it developed 150bhp at 11,000 rpm and Kawamoto applied its principles to the 3-litre V-12 he drew up for the 1966 Formula One. It had the same ratio of bore to stroke, much the same valve gear and, although it did not provide three times the power, its 400bhp was enough to be competitive.

A mock-up of the 1.5-litre Honda transverse Formula One engine was sent to Lotus at Cheshunt for fitting in an experimental chassis, but the project foundered. Chapman, it seems, was interested only in putting pressure on Coventry-Climax to produce something with more power that he could have on better terms. How different it might have been if the deal had gone through. The Formula Two Brabhams won not only their first race at Goodwood, but the next 10 races in a row in 1966 while Chapman's hoped-for Coventry-Climax flat-16 engine was stillborn and he had nothing ready for the 3-litre formula until the Ford-Cosworth of 1967 created by Ford expressly for Jim Clark to win the world championship. Had Chapman worked with Honda – which showed its mettle by winning the final race of the 1.5-litre formula in Mexico in 1965 – what progress might have been made for 1966.

Rewarding work. The successful Brabham-Honda F2 car of 1964 (below)

Bucknum
at the
Nürburgring
(right):
the ill-starred
German Grand
Prix of 1964

Yoshio
Nakamura
(below right)
under-
estimated the
opposition

It was a quarter of a century before such a combination of the world's best driver, the world's best engine, and the world's best car would happen again.

After the bruising experience with Chapman, Honda knew it would have to build its own car. It was not an appealing prospect but there was little choice, and following several years' seasoning in motorcycle racing it knew there were two means of choosing drivers. Established stars would not only demand premium fees, they would grow disgruntled if they failed to win, yet only they were capable of telling Honda if it had a winning car. Dan Gurney and Phil Hill said they were unavailable for 1964, so Honda picked a driver unknown outside American west coast club racing. Cynics suggested it was to allow for the possibility of defeat which could always be blamed on a new and inexperienced driver. Ronnie Bucknum was 28, worked as a surveyor, and raced an Austin-Healey and an MGB. Would he care to test a Formula One Honda at the Nürburgring? Within months the gallant young American was on the starting grid of the German Grand Prix on the 14-mile roller-coaster track in the heart of the Eifel Mountains.

It was a brave effort all round. The 60 degree V-12 engine of the RA271 was a radical design mounted transversely behind the driver, which shortened the wheelbase but increased the frontal area. The overhead camshafts and four valves per cylinder left space for only one NGK spark plug along the lines of the 250cc four-cylinder racing motorcycle. The exhausts of the front bank of cylinders ran underneath the engine to emerge just ahead of the rear wheel centres, and the six twin-choke Keihin carburettors were soon replaced by Keihin-Honda indirect fuel

injection that brought the power output to 220bhp at 11,000rpm.

The engine, six-speed gearbox, and final drive were in one unit, the gearbox ahead of the rear wheels and the drive taken from the middle of the crankshaft, making the engine in effect two stiff V-6s, once again following motorcycle practice as exemplified by Gilera and MV.

It was not an auspicious start. The team was badly prepared despite running test sessions at Zandvoort, Holland, and a great deal was expected of the first Japanese entry in a world championship grand prix. Honda's splendid record in motorcycle racing prompted Denis Jenkinson of *Motor Sport* to write: "The four-cylinder Honda motorcycle made a big impression and the production sports and mopeds have continued the good name made by racing, but we must not forget that Honda racing motorcycles started in a very inconspicuous manner and progressed as the seasons went by. They did not appear on the scene and win immediately."

Jenkinson recognised that Honda started by contesting classes where the opposition was weak, but this was not an option against Lotus, BRM, Brabham, Ferrari, and Coventry-Climax. No weakness here and grand prix racing was full of classic makes with world championships recently under their belt, such as Cooper. Even Porsche found it difficult to keep up the pace and won only one victory before pulling out at the end of 1965. Soichiro Honda radiated confidence in an interview with the distinguished German journalist Günther Molter in 1962: "It is too early to talk of horsepower as the project is still at the development stage. I can tell you that our grand prix car will have an engine performance unequalled by any of the known makes of Formula One grand prix cars."

TADASHI KUME

Honda was not Kume's first choice, but he failed a competing company's entrance examination and took advice from his professor at Shizuoka University from which he graduated in engineering. "The Honda exam is easier," he was told. He passed it and almost at once in April 1953 was set the task of designing motorcycle racing engines.

Kume was responsible for the twin-cam four-cylinder, 350cc engine of the T360 truck and S360 sports car. Like the later Formula One engine, the sports car stuck to racing motorcycle practice with a carburettor for each cylinder. It was exquisite and no reflection on Kume that it was discarded and developed into something bigger when he returned to the competition department.

Kume went on to evolve the hugely successful Formula Two engine for Jack Brabham in the 1960s but was thwarted by

Soichiro Honda from making a suitable Formula One engine with Kawamoto for John Surtees in 1967-1968.

He was recruited by Soichiro to take part in development of the ill-starred RA302 grand prix engine and then the unsuccessful 1300 saloon (left), but eventually led the opposition to the president's air-cooled fixation although not before quitting and being reinstated by Kawashima.

Kume took charge of Honda in 1983, remaining president and chief executive until Nobuhiko Kawamoto took over in 1990.

The clean lines of Honda's first grand prix car, driven by Ronnie Bucknum at the Nürburgring (right)

Exposed. Valve gear of the forward bank of the V-12 engine (below right)

Soichiro's "known makes" had dazzling V-8s from BRM and Coventry-Climax, V-6s, V-8s, and flat-12s from Ferrari, and an air-cooled flat-8 from Porsche. Honda produced its radical little V-12 with needle roller crankshaft bearings revving to 11,500rpm, in a semi-monocoque chassis with suspension that owed something to Lotus and BRM tubular rear sub-frames and inboard springs. The transverse engine mounting owed nothing to anybody however, and lived up to Soichiro's assurances with 20bhp more than any of its rivals, including the Ferrari flat-12. The little V-12 was a triumph for Kume, a mechanical engineering graduate, plunged into the design of racing motorcycle engines even though relatively inexperienced.

"Nobody at Honda really expected the car to shatter the racing world at its first appearance but such was the publicity accrued from motorcycle racing that the grand prix car was preceded by almost fanatical expectations emanating from Europe rather than Japan," according to Jenkinson. The reason for the established teams' apprehension was the proficiency Honda showed at high-revving engines with large numbers of small cylinders and four-valve heads. Ferrari was notably successful with V-12s, and Coventry-Climax, also an acknowledged master of the racing engine craft, had a 16-cylinder under development. Accordingly, Honda was half-expected to have a roller-bearing 16 of its own with prodigious power.

Jenkinson's admiration for Honda was not shared throughout Europe. Italians complained that Kume's masterpiece resembled an engine designed by Giulio Alfieri for Maserati in 1961, test-bedded in 1963 but only made public in 1964 after the Honda.

Yet if the prevailing teams overestimated Honda's prospects, Nakamura probably underestimated theirs. Honda's 1964 offensive lacked the refinement and style of the motorcycle

The pits, Nürburgring (left). West German crowds assess the new car

Monaco 1965. Richie Ginther brakes hard for the Tabac, (below centre) and concentrates at the hairpin (below)

racing department's, the cars were a year late and never had the polished finish of a Lotus nor the glamorous appearance of a Ferrari. It was 1965 before they started to gain a competitive edge, an achievement that had eluded Porsche, but given the expectations raised by the exquisite motorcycles, it was scarcely any less than had been expected.

The 1964 German Grand Prix, Bucknum's debut, was a disaster. The team scarcely knew the rules of grand prix racing and had to install an oil catch-tank at the circuit, a famously undignified Coca-Cola can wired on to the back, with plastic pipes. The car was not fast enough, and in practice the engine failed to run cleanly so the luckless Bucknum started at the back of the grid a minute slower than John Surtees' best time, in a V-8 Ferrari, of 9min 38.4sec on the longest, toughest track in motor racing. It was a serious deficit and although once the race began the brave Bucknum overtook eight cars, on lap 12 the steering broke and he went off the road, fortunately without injury.

Matters improved at the Italian Grand Prix in September. The long straights on the Monza track invited slipstreaming, where a driver pulling up close behind a faster car could speed up in the aerodynamic wake. By pulling out at the right moment he could even overtake. Bucknum was able to prove the car a match for the opposition by overtaking several cars without the need to use this slipstreaming "tow". The Honda had sufficient power to get by without it, so whatever else was wrong, the car was not short of raw energy. Bucknum made a poor start from the middle of the race grid, but worked his way up to fifth before retiring with overheating and brake trouble.

Honda won great credit for not waiting – as Mercedes-Benz might have done – until meticulous testing proved it competitive. Instead it raced in the full glare of publicity, doing its testing and development as it went, conscious that nothing would compel its engineers to learn faster than the rough and tumble of competition.

The Honda lasted 50 laps of the United States Grand Prix at Watkins Glen but clearly Bucknum's work was done, and a more experienced development driver who knew how

Eau Rouge, 1965 Belgian Grand Prix (right). Graham Hill's BRM hides Jim Clark's winning Lotus-Climax, followed by Jackie Stewart (BRM), Richie Ginther (Honda), Jo Siffert (Brabham-BRM), John Surtees (Ferrari), Dan Gurney (Brabham), Bruce McLaren (Cooper-Climax), Jo Bonnier (Brabham-Climax) and Ronnie Bucknum (Honda). Ginther finished sixth behind Stewart, McLaren, Brabham, and Hill

Mexico City,
24 October,
1965. Richie
Ginther takes
the chequered
flag for his sole,
and Honda's
first grand prix
victory (below,
right)

With Yoshio
Nakamura
celebrating
(below)

a grand prix car should behave was sought for 1965. Richie Ginther had been a serviceable test driver for Ferrari and BRM and, although scarcely in the top flight of grand prix competitors, he knew how to describe a racing car's behaviour to engineers. More important, he was able to assess the value of the changes they made. BRM's team manager and chief engineer, Tony Rudd, described Ginther as sensitive and observant, an invaluable development driver, and thus exactly what Nakamura needed. He was also a consistent driver, measured and capable, and although gaining only two sixth places before winning the final race of the season in Mexico, his contribution to Honda's historic victory in only its ninth grand prix was substantial.

The 1965 RA272 car looked much the same as the one Bucknum drove in 1964, but its engine was mounted in a tubular sub-frame and, following the stuttering misfirings of its first season, ran cleanly to 14,000rpm. Its output of 240bhp at 11,000rpm made it the most powerful engine of the 1.5-litre era, even though it produced its most useful pulling power only within a narrow rev range which tested a driver's concentration. There was no revving high and hoping for the best; it had to be operated within disciplined limits.

The season again began inauspiciously with a back-of-the-grid start on the street circuit at Monaco and a first-lap retirement. At the next race, the Belgian Grand Prix at Spa, Ginther finished sixth. Both cars retired from the French Grand Prix on the hilly Charade Circuit at Clermont-Ferrand, but Honda's days of glory began when Ginther shared the front row of the grid on the former airfield at Silverstone with Jim Clark (Lotus), Graham Hill (BRM), and Jackie Stewart (BRM). Starting alongside the stars showed what the car was capable of and Honda fairly came of age on Silverstone's long straights, demonstrating, as it had the year before at Monza, that it was a force to be reckoned with, and making good Soichiro's promise to Günther Molter that the car would have more power than given by any known make of grand prix engine. Ginther even snatched the lead on the first lap but retired with engine failure.

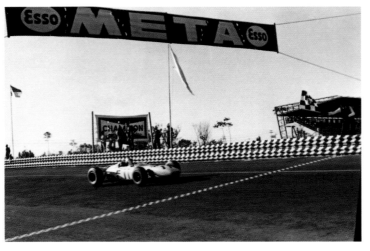

By 1966 the
Honda V-12
engine was
mounted
longways in
the frame.
Richie Ginther's
car at Monza
with the
exhausts
sprouting from
the middle of
the Vee (right)

In the opening laps of the Dutch Grand Prix, among the
dunes of the windy seaside resort of Zandvoort, Ginther once
again led briefly and finished sixth. The team missed the German
Grand Prix at the Nürburgring so there was no repeat of 1964's
fiasco, but nor was there any echo of the promise shown at
Monza in the Italian Grand Prix where Ginther was 4 seconds
a lap down in practice and retired after 57 laps. In the golden
autumn of upstate New York, he started well in the United
States Grand Prix at Watkins Glen, but was lapped twice and
finished seventh.

The final race of 1965 was the last of the 1.5-litre grand prix
formula that had been the rule since 1961. An undistinguished
formula in respect of speed and spectacular cars, it nevertheless
provided close racing and was about to be replaced by a
maximum capacity of 3-litres or 1.5-litres supercharged. The
7,000ft altitude for the Mexican Grand Prix left some engines
rather breathless, starved of oxygen. The Mexico City track's
S-bends put a premium on handling, and the Hondas ran well
from the first day of practice.

In the race Ginther took the lead from the second row of
the grid behind Jim Clark (Lotus-Climax) and Dan Gurney
(Brabham-Climax), and by the end of the first lap he was 300
yards ahead. "I looked in my mirror and I just didn't see a soul
until I was clear past the end of the pits. I thought I might have
dropped oil on the track and they'd all spun out," Ginther said.
Gurney never got closer than two seconds behind his fellow
American, who had plenty in reserve and never had to rev
above 11,000rpm. Honda was making history. It was the first
victory by a Japanese car since the dawn of grand prix racing in
1906 and, as well as being the final race of the 1.5-litre formula,
it was also the first grand prix victory for Goodyear tyres.

Ginther leads
into Copse in
the 1965
British Grand
Prix from the
front row of
the grid ahead
of Clark, Hill,
and Stewart.
(overleaf)

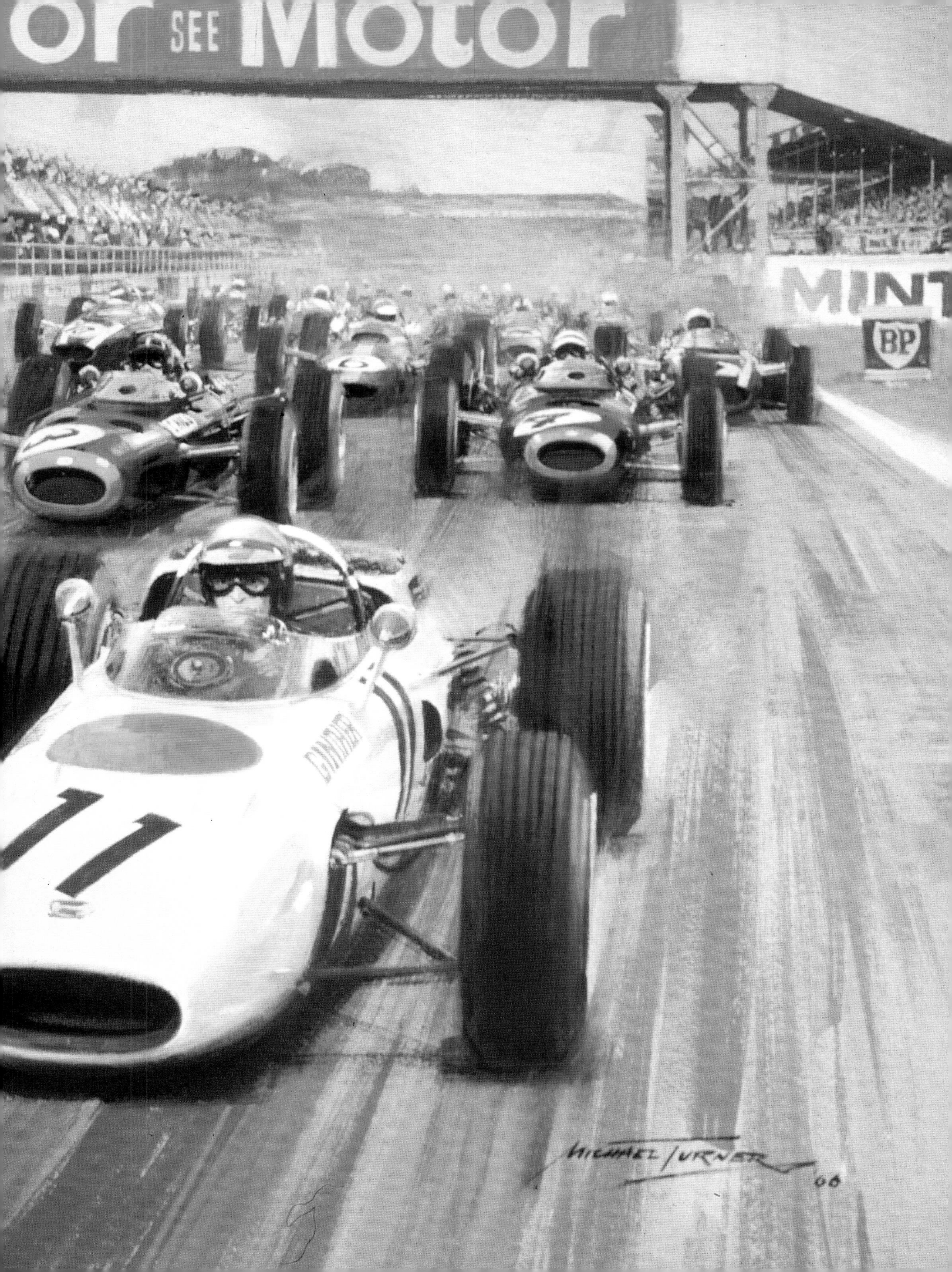
or SEE Motor
MINT
BP
11

Denny Hulme
in the Formula
Two Brabham-
Honda at
Rouen. The
F2 engine's
seventh victory
of 1966 (right)

Start of the
Italian Grand
Prix at Monza
(below).
Jack Brabham
(Repco-
Brabham)
cooly adjusts
his mirror.
Winner
Surtees
(Honda) is
the white car
in tenth place

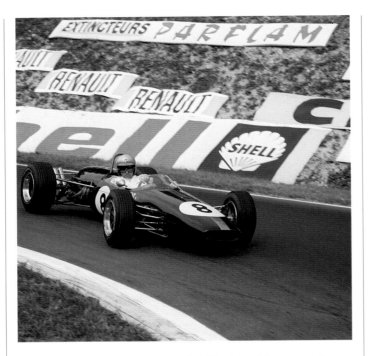

The first engine designed by Soichiro Irimajiri to meet the
new Formula One regulations was overweight. After the
spectacular victory in Mexico a great deal was now expected
of Honda, bearing out Jenkinson's view that the team would
start modestly but had the talent and proficiency to overwhelm
the opposition. Yet the new V-12 not only weighed more than
600kg, it was short of power and with the minimum weight limit
for the entire car at 500kg, the prospects were not encouraging.

Against rivals with 350bhp, the RA273 developed 400bhp at
10,000rpm and although it revved freely and noisily it was never
in contention. Beautifully engineered with the same central
power take-off as the 1.5-litre, which again made it resemble
two stiff little 90-degree V-6s with four valves per cylinder and
a roller bearing crankshaft, it was not ready until late 1966.
Installed conventionally behind the driver in line with the chassis
this time, the engine contributed substantially to the car's all-up
weight on the Monza weighbridge of 743kg. Ginther was well
up in the early stages of the Italian Grand Prix but a puncture led
to an accident and he crashed heavily. It was almost the last time
the car looked competitive. The combination of its high weight
and unreliability made changes inevitable and urgent.

Honda was not alone in its anxiety. The 3-litre formula was
something of a conundrum for designers uncertain how
to evaluate power against weight. BRM's complex H-16 was
heavy, and not only short of power but short of reliability too.
Coventry-Climax withdrew, Ferrari needed more time for
development, Cooper's heavy Maserati engine was a stop-gap,
Lotus's new Ford-Cosworth unready, and the Gurney Eagle-
Weslake insufficiently powerful.

Kume's response for 1967, in concert with Nobuhiko
Kawamoto, was the RA300. Yoshio Nakamura recruited John
Surtees by joining up with Team Surtees, which had been set

up to race a Lola sports car. Fresh from his 1964 world championship and a fruitful if sometimes acrimonious spell with Ferrari, Surtees was driver, technician, and strategist. There was no doubt about his enthusiasm and will to win – Honda had a high regard for his abilities and his track record spoke for itself but his multiple roles and the long lines of communication between Europe and Japan, in the days before fax machines, track telemetry, and satellite telephones, created serious difficulties.

The season began with the RA273 but the weight problem persisted. "It was built like the Forth Bridge," according to Surtees. "The engine was heavy, but it was interesting in the 1980s to see Porsche use the same central power take-off for its Formula One V-12 as Honda had."

Surtees was unhappy with progress towards lightening the car, so working with Soichi Sano, Honda's project engineer, and Eric Broadley, whose Lola Engineering was close by Team Surtees at Slough, he pressed forward using a Lola Indianapolis monocoque as the basis for a lighter, slimmer car designed with the V-12 engine in a tubular sub-frame. It was not as light as expected, despite saving 100lb or so with titanium components made specially in Japan. "A waste of time," according to Jenkinson. "It was clear that the whole conception of the car was wrong. When Colin Chapman tackled Indianapolis in 1964 he demanded an engine that gave 1bhp for every 1lb weight. Without that it was not worth his while starting the project. He got a 350lb engine giving 350bhp." It made Honda's 1,320lb engine with just over 400bhp seem less than adequate.

The central power take-off carried the penalty of a heavy three-shaft gearbox. "We were not steaming away from the opposition down the straights. It took Honda a long time to

Honda happy hunting ground, Mexico City (right). Richie Ginther (Honda) leads the first lap of the grand prix from Jochen Rindt (Cooper-Maserati), and Jack Brabham (Repco-Brabham). Winner, No 7, on the right, was John Surtees (Cooper-Maserati). Ginther finished fourth

A deft touch of opposite lock as John Surtees (Honda) turns on to the sea-front at Portier in the 1968 Monaco Grand Prix (right)

Weeping weather. Rouen. Surtees passes the spot where Jo Schlesser died in the French Grand Prix (far right)

The centre-exhaust V-12 Formula One engine (below)

JOHN SURTEES

Winner of seven world championships on bikes, one in cars with Ferrari, John Surtees hoped for more than a solitary grand prix victory when he drove for Honda in 1967 and 1968. The first season began promisingly enough with third place in the South African Grand Prix at Kyalami followed by three retirements with engine problems. Surtees was sixth in the British and fourth in the German before winning at Monza with the Honda-Lola; then things deteriorated again.

The second year was little better, with the best result ironically in the tragic rain-drenched French Grand Prix at Rouen, and although unhappy that development of a Kume/Kawamoto lightweight compact V-12 was halted by Soichiro Honda, Surtees was not completely dissatisfied. "The season had not yielded victories, but we'd shown promise. I was easily leading the Belgian Grand Prix at Spa when a rear suspension bracket – made in England, unfortunately – broke. I ran with the leaders at Monza before going off on oil dropped by Chris Amon's Ferrari. It was the end of two wasted years, yet paradoxically it was also the beginning of a new Honda."

Monza 1967.
The 'Hondola'
in the Italian
Grand Prix
(above)

learn the value of useable mid-range power and torque of
the kind demonstrated by the Cosworth DFV," said the driver-
technician.

The best 1967 result was an encouraging victory at Monza,
a last-lap sprint to the line in one of the most dramatic grand
prix races of modern times, taking place at the very heart of
Italian motor racing. Honda at last won its position among the
classic makes, but for Surtees it was only a step towards an
elusive goal and he remained edgy.

"After giving the matter considerable thought and once again
being ruled by my heart rather than my head," he wrote later,
"I considered what Honda had achieved in motorcycle racing.
What I hadn't bargained for was the way in which the Japanese
would behave. I was about to enter a political situation rather
similar to that which I had experienced with Ferrari and, just
as I felt we were on the verge of producing a really competitive
machine, based round a lightweight V-12, the whole project was
quashed at the end of 1968 after Soichiro Honda went off at
a tangent with the air/oil-cooled RA302 V-8 in which poor Jo
Schlesser was killed in the French Grand Prix."

The Grand Prix de l'Automobile Club de France, as it was
still called, took place at Rouen the week the air-cooled N360
saloon car was being introduced in France. Soichiro Honda was
in Paris at the time launching it, and prompted Honda France
to nominate Schlesser, 40 years of age and in the twilight of his
racing career, to drive in the grand prix. He had been up against
the best drivers of the day in Formula Two and even taken part
in the Formula Two category of the German Grands Prix of
1966 and 1967, but he had never driven a full-blown Formula
One car in a race.

The move to air-cooling stemmed from Honda's years of
success with air-cooled motorcycles. Kume did not much like
the idea because of localised overheating in the 120 degree V-8,
but he got down to work with the RA302 none the less. It was
not the only air-cooled Formula One engine; the 1.5-litre
Porsche Type 753 was also an air-cooled 8-cylinder with four
overhead camshafts and ironically it was at Rouen-les-Essarts,
this same track, and driven by Dan Gurney, that it won its only

With Clark out of fuel, Surtees wrong-footed Brabham on the last corner to snatch victory in the 1967 Italian Grand Prix (left)

High wings. David Hobbs (Honda, below) was lying sixth in the 1968 Italian Grand Prix when a valve dropped into the engine

world championship race, the 1962 French Grand Prix.

Surtees protested that the engine was overheating as expected, but intended to drive the car in practice and see how it behaved. He had already driven it at Silverstone, rejected any idea of racing it, but expected development to carry on in secret until the autumn. When he got to Rouen however, he was astonished to find a rival Honda team with a different set of mechanics and he was concerned about Schlesser's inexperience. The Frenchman lost control on the third lap on a fast downhill sweep. The car was still brim-full of fuel, overturned and caught fire immediately, and Schlesser died in flames made more intense by the magnesium used in the structure.

The RA302 deserved better. It was one of the most innovative cars in the early stages of the 3-litre formula, with an engine at the beginning of its development producing 385bhp

at 9,000rpm. Honda racing motorcycles were developing 160bhp per litre, so a 480bhp 3-litre was clearly within reach. Nominally air-cooled, it used airflow through the engine to keep down oil temperature. There was a high rate of oil flow round the engine to cool the cylinder heads, and air circulated through the crankcase mingling with the oil mist before being blown out the back, an arrangement that echoed Soichiro Honda's ill-starred 1300 saloon. There was a short magnesium-skinned monocoque with the front suspension mounted on a forward bulkhead, and the engine hung from a backbone extending from the rear bulkhead.

John Surtees finished second at Rouen in a water-cooled RA301, essentially an improved RA300 with slimmer monocoque and a revised engine with the ingenious torsion bar valve springs developed by Kume for Brabham's brilliantly successful Formula Two engine. But the fiery accident stained Honda's reputation in Formula One and it withdrew from racing at the end of 1968.

Kume declared: "Our concern about air pollution reached a peak and the engineers' attention had to be turned to ways of reducing emissions. This did not leave us much time for racing." The internal arguments about air-cooling and water-cooling continued however, Kume maintaining that water-cooling was important for stable combustion temperatures and for high power as well as low emissions. Soichiro Honda was stubborn and the two fell out. Kume left and retired to the island of Shikoku to think things over until Kawashima persuaded him to return. Takeo Fujisawa was the only person who could get Soichiro to see the error of his ways, leave the engineers to get on with things and reinstate Kume. In due course Soichiro did just that, but the altercation had a lasting effect on the company.

Team Surtees and Lola Cars co-operated in the creation of a winning Honda (above)

Mexico, 1968 (right). Surtees (Honda), second on the opening lap, went out with overheating.

March 1973.
The
Experimental
Safety Vehicle
(ESV) with
impact-
absorbing
bumpers and
CVCC engine
(below)

Cylinder head
secrets in the
CVCC engine
(below)

CVCC and VTEC

In February 1971, Compound Vortex Controlled Combustion (CVCC) was an imaginative engineering response to pending United States emission control legislation. It used Honda's deep knowledge of the combustion process to design an engine that burnt fuel cleanly, because Honda took the view that it was better to cremate the pollutants inside the engine rather than clean them off in the exhaust pipe afterwards.

Fuel/air mixtures were not easy to ignite smoothly unless the blend was right - around 15 parts air to one part petrol was the goal. Engines running

a rich 10 parts of air were throwing a good deal of unburnt fuel into the atmosphere to make smog. Weaker mixtures were difficult to burn smoothly unless part of the stream (a stratum) was enriched to ignite the remainder.

Stratified charge aimed to achieve total burning of the fuel with a lean mixture of 17 or 18 parts air. A small high-temperature pre-combustion chamber set off the larger, weaker portion

of the mixture. The cool-running engine which resulted generated less nitrogen oxides, and, because it drew in more oxygen, produced less carbon monoxide. Honda oxidised the extra hydrocarbons with a new exhaust manifold and the CVCC was greeted with enthusiasm by engineers, by the United States National Academy of Science, and by environmentalists.

CVCC gave Honda a significant lead in emissions study, but it was something of a Pyrrhic victory. Exhaust emission regulations were sacrificed to political expediency, often running contrary to the best scientific and technical advice. Politicians set the wrong agenda, leading engineers to pursue the wrong aims. Exhaust cleansing was adopted instead of the purer solution of combustion efficiency.

Only Honda and Toyo Kogyo, the makers of Mazdas, succeeded in meeting the regulations. The National Academy of Sciences in America commended the CVCC system, which it said was years ahead of anything else as well as being first to meet the 1975 standards. It drew world-wide attention and gained awards in many countries. The technology was bought by Toyota, Ford, Isuzu, Chrysler, among others, but Japanese manufactures and the American motor industry delayed the progress of the legislation until the preferred solution became catalytic converters, effectively making CVCC unnecessary.

Honda had more luck with Variable Valve Timing and Lift Electronic Control (VTEC), which effectively transformed the engine from three-valve (best for economy) to four-valve (for extra power) automatically. An elegant solution to the conflicting requirements of economy, speed, and low exhaust emissions, it disengaged one of the inlet valves when the car was driven slowly. The air then entered the cylinder fast and swirled quickly for lean

burning. Economy was improved and emissions reduced.

At about 2,500rpm on full throttle – higher for partial throttle openings – the hydraulic link-pins in the valve gear, prompted by electronic controls monitoring the air-fuel ratio, brought the idle valve into play and altered valve timing and lift. The changeover to the "alternative engine" was imperceptible.

Fujisawa was dismayed to find that Honda Motor had been unable to take more practical advantage of its leadership in racing engine design so convincingly established in Formula Two. "Scoring 12 victories in a season was unprecedented. Those engines incorporated technology which ought to have been more readily transferred to production car engines. We had mastered the techniques for building car bodies, yet we failed to transfer the expertise from racing to road car engines."

Work began on the CVCC stratified charge engine which met strict American emission limits with a year to spare. It was a triumph for Honda's research and development, well ahead of the rest of the world's motor industry which still claimed the legislation was impossible to meet, yet Fujisawa was not satisfied with progress. Honda took 15 years to get into car manufacturing, but its development into a world-class producer took the best part of another 10 years. It made 136 vehicles in 1963, 5,210 in 1964, and 8,779 in 1965 of which around a quarter were exported. It was 1966 before it began to make real progress, falling back to 3,209 before making a breakthrough only in 1967 with 87,000. The key was a strong home market on which to build up to 186,500 in 1968 and 232,000 in 1969, of which a mere 5.4 per cent were exported.

The first tentative production models were the S500 sports car and T360 truck, followed by the evolutionary S600 coupe and in October 1965 the L700 estate car. The S500 gave Honda its first taste of four-wheeled competition when left-hand-drive cars were entered for the 1964 Spa-Sofia-Liege rally, and an S600 driven by Denny Hulme won its class in the ADAC 600kms endurance race at the Nürburgring in September 1964, giving Honda its first victory in a car race.

VTEC cast into a cam cover of the NSX (above left) and swirling the charge in the combustion chamber of the four-valve head (left)

The T360 truck (right) was Honda's first four wheeler in 1963. Later versions had snow-tracks, flatbed bodies

HONDA S800

Introduced at the Tokyo motor show in November 1962 the Sports 360 and 500 were essentially miniature two-seaters analogous to a contemporary MG or Austin-Healey. Unlike the Fiat 850 Spyder of 1965 with the engine behind the driver and elegant styling by Bertone, the Honda broke little new ground in appearance or layout. Its designers stuck conservatively to an engine in front driving the rear wheels, yet the car was manufactured with watch-making precision. In 1962 an inclined aluminium hemi-head four-cylinder with a roller bearing crank and twin overhead camshafts was the stuff of extravagantly expensive sports or racing cars. A Keihin carburettor for each cylinder was a legacy of Honda's racing motorcycles and although the S360 never went into production, the 531cc S500 was made until 1964 when it was supplanted by the 606cc S600. The open two-seater body style was augmented by a fastback coupe, and when the S800 appeared at the 1965 Tokyo motor show it was available in both styles.

Introduced in the wake of Honda's success in motorcycle racing, and in Europe at the same time as the firm was dominating small-capacity Formula Two racing, the S800 looked a certain winner.

It had independent suspension with wishbones and torsion bars at the front, precise rack and pinion steering, and a simple box-section ladder frame with lots of cross-bracing and four outriggers for the body mountings. When it was announced for Japan it had a novel arrangement at the back with enclosed chain drives that formed trailing arms for the independently sprung rear wheels. It was a layout similar to a sprint car built by Raymond Mays in 1949 that turned out to be uncontrollable, but the Honda had better fortune. Its road performance was highly

satisfactory with the little engine kept spinning at high revs by abundant use of the gearbox. The brakes were never quite up to the job until discs were introduced at the front, and although the four-speed gearbox had synchromesh throughout, it was no longer clash-proof when the oil was thoroughly warmed.

It was a jewel of a car. Although a modest 791cc, it generated 70bhp at 8,000 rpm, revving safely to 11,000 rpm and giving 88.5bhp per litre when the cast iron pushrod engine shared by contemporary Austin-Healey Sprites and MG Midgets was struggling to make 50bhp at

4,500 rpm and threatening to blow itself asunder at 6,000 rpm. The Honda was a model of smoothness and refinement, well ahead of the opposition technically, and for a time it seemed likely to repeat Honda's motorcycle accomplishments.

Yet it was less than an outstanding success in Britain. Between 1967 and April 1970 1,548 were imported, all with a conventional live rear axle instead of chain drive, and even though it was well-made and reliable compared with

outmoded European rivals, competitively priced, and adequately stylish, 500 cars a year was not much against the Sprite and Midget's combined - although declining – 20,000.

The S800 was small. Strapping young Europeans who made up the bulk of sports car buyers found the cockpit cramped and the luggage space less than adequate. Sports cars were used for practical touring as well as club competitions and the Mini-Cooper was a new rival to the traditional two-seater. Its astonishing front-wheel drive cornering made it more than a match even for the nimble Honda which was also scarcely fast despite its

willingness to rev. Road tests gave it a top speed of 94mph and 0-60mph acceleration in 13.6sec, almost identical to the contemporary Austin-Healey Sprite IV and a good deal slower than a Mini-Cooper S 1275.

The difficulty of meeting Californian emission regulations, high noise levels, and limited accommodation led to the demise of the S800. It cost £779 in 1967, just over £100 dearer than a Sprite or Midget and £62 more than a Triumph Spitfire, yet £140 less

than the larger MGB. Fuel consumption of 27mpg was unexceptional although, since it only used two-star fuel – most unusual for a sports car – it was not regarded as uneconomical.

Motor Sport said: "The S800's eagerness and responsiveness is enhanced by an engine that not only sounds and runs like something out of a motor race, but which develops real power." The hood was watertight, the range short owing to a niggardly 7.7-gallon fuel tank, but even though it failed to make a deep impression on the market, it had a lasting influence on the destiny of the European sports car.

Recipe for success. TT wins on two wheels, a carburettor for every cylinder. Open and closed S800s delighted sports car enthusiasts (above and right)

In March 1967 came the N360 mini sub-compact with a four-stroke twin-cylinder 354cc engine which revved to a resounding 8,500rpm to produce 31bhp. It had front-wheel drive, did 71mph and, astonishingly, it was also available as a three-speed automatic with a torque converter. Nakamura encouraged the project as suitable for the young generation of Japanese car-buyer to graduate to from Honda Cubs, and the style and the front-wheel drive owed something to the Issigonis Mini. Soichiro approved of front wheel drive. "A bullock cart is very stable round corners, and it has its power source at the front", he said. Yet for Japan it was revolutionary, and was in a good position to take advantage of the 1960s minicar boom.

Soichiro's enthusiasm for air-cooling was becoming something of an obsession and the celebrated disagreement over the Formula One car extended to road cars beyond the little N360 and its successor of July 1968, the N600. His engineers knew how he had pressed ahead with the Honda 1300 in the mid-1960s against their better judgment. Finally launched in May 1969, it had an air-cooled engine of 100bhp and novel design. It was a car that promised much but was a showroom failure and effectively ended Soichiro Honda's career as a car designer.

It looked like most middle-sized Japanese cars of the time with a front grille like a Morris Marina and had the boxy elegance of a small Fiat. It did 110mph and reached 7,200rpm, had front-wheel drive, a transverse engine, disc brakes, and DDAC (Dual-Dyna Air Cooling) to tackle the noise problem of air-cooled engines with an elaborate ducting system and cooling fins designed not to resonate. The 1300 was as quiet as a 2CV Citroën, said Honda. The outside of the cylinders was cooled by ambient airflow, and a fan also blew air through the interior down sealed ducts over fins cast in the cylinders and cylinder heads. It had dry-sump lubrication and was successfully quiet but, notwithstanding its use of many expensive aluminium components, it exceeded its weight target of 800kgs by 130kgs. The engine was large, heavy, costly, and mounted so far forward that the car understeered badly. Driven fast it felt twitchy and nervous. The company lost money on every 1300 it sold and although Fujisawa was prepared to acknowledge its technical merit he knew that Honda Motor could not go on like that.

He went along with the introduction of a sleek coupe version in 1970 which sold quite well, but the saloon was a commercial flop. It was replaced with the water-cooled 145 which looked the same and was scarcely any more of a success.

Kiyoshi Kawashima led the campaign against air-cooling largely on the grounds that water-cooling was indispensable for the even combustion chamber temperatures necessary to meet the approaching emission regulations. Kawashima counselled Fujisawa on the risks Soichiro was running, and the two chiefs met over dinner in the autumn of 1969 to settle the matter. They had not seen each other for some time and Fujisawa's mind was made up. "If Mr Honda refuses to make a water-cooled engine this means he is following a different path from

Mini-compact of the 1960s. The N360 four-stroke twin-cylinder took Honda into new trade (top, left)

Coupe version of the hapless 1300 saloon, stylish but imperfect (below, left)

mine. If the two of us cannot go in the same direction our teamwork will not function." He gave Soichiro an ultimatum. He could continue as president (Honda Motor tried to avoid the title chairman – Soichiro was president, Fujisawa executive vice-president) only by allowing his engineers to work on water-cooled engines, which they had been doing secretly in any case.

Soichiro at length agreed, but it was said in Honda R&D that he never allowed himself to smile when discussing water-cooling, and for their part the engineers henceforth asserted that water-cooling was only invoked to make their engines run smoothly and quietly. Soichiro had to give in and commented wryly on it when he drove the first water-cooled prototype one rainy, cold, November afternoon on the test track. He stopped the little car, got out, and remarked on the warmth conferred by the water-circulated interior heater.

"Perhaps air-cooling represented the limit of my technology," he said later. The result of the imbroglio was two-fold. It resulted in autonomy for the R&D division of Honda Motor and created a corporate culture which transcended individuals at every level. Soichiro was confirmed as president, which he remained until taking on his virtually honorary role of supreme adviser in 1973. Fujisawa adopted a similar function, and together they agreed to hand the company on to a new generation.

Soichiro was always adamant that Honda Motor did not belong to the Honda family and believed that his authority was a necessary counter-balance to the egalitarianism within the company. The founders' rule about not allowing their direct family to enter the firm even in the lower ranks was later extended to every member of the board. Honda's philosophy that every member of the company was equal, and the only difference was the role they played and the salary they obtained, continued throughout the corporation whenever new offices or plants were opened.

Fujisawa blamed himself for letting the 1300 programme get out of control. "I did not make a perfect decision," he said later. "There was insufficient discussion about whether the car should be air-cooled or water-cooled. I did not listen to the engineers until it was too late. If we had chosen an alternative course

The innovative Z360 of 1970 (above). Talent for good proportions and stylish practicality starts to show

OUTBOARD ENGINES

Modern outboard engines were a far cry from the recalcitrant, noisy, smoky, and unreliable machines that once dangled astern of small boats, and represented not so much a useful means of propulsion as a step up the evolutionary ladder from rowing. Their development was aimed at power, economy and reliability, but by the 1990s the marine environment became a priority.

Some waterways had become sources of drinking water and in any case pollution by oil or exhaust gases was no longer acceptable. The Bodensee in Germany led the way in laying down strict emission and noise levels and Hondas were the first, – and for some time the only – engines to meet them.

Honda only ever made four-stroke outboards, and its latter-day vertically-mounted cross-flow engines had electronic controls and exhaust outlets in the propellor hub. The 9.9 and 15 were also the world's first outboards with Dr Lanchester's balancer shafts, as used in the car engines, to smooth out vibrations.

Foaming brine. Quiet, clean Honda outboards show their paces (left)

Civics came in variety of guises including the 1974 Wagon (far right)

Second coming. The 1982 improved Prelude (far right, bottom)

The Tochigi test facility (below), completed in 1979, contained the specialist NSX factory

earlier, the company would probably have made a much greater leap forward at a time when the Japanese industry was entering a period of rapid growth that may never be repeated. Honda Motor expanded through the priority it gave to technology, but there are times when management must take priority over technology".

It was too late to stop the 1970 Z Life based on the small saloon series but, although Soichiro's air-cooled fixation was ultimately unsuccessful, the cars it generated turned out to be the foundation of a brilliant range. The nascent Civic could be detected in the Z Life; the related Ballade and the grown-up Accord in the 1300; and the Prelude in the elegant styling of the 1970 Coupe. The 1971 Life came out with a water-cooled twin-cylinder engine but flagging sales of the N360 and the heavy cost of the 1300 meant that the profits of the motorcycle division had to prop up the car side.

By 1973 the Civic was well on its way, its CVCC ahead of American emission control regulations ensuring its place in the United States market. Three-quarters of all two- and four-door Civics were exported (by 1979 production was 706,375 cars a year), and by the second half of the 1970s the turnover of Honda cars exceeded that of the motorcycle division. The reorganised R&D department meanwhile was aglow with new ideas. The Tochigi proving ground was finished in 1979, the Civic was improved and came out as an estate car, called a van, as a technical collaboration agreement was signed with British Leyland. New products followed thick and fast in the 1980s, the Paris-Dakar replica XL250R motorcycle, the CBX400F Integra, 750F Integra, and new Ballade and Civics in 1982. Honda of America began production of the Accord in Marysville, Ohio, and in November 1982 came the sleekest Honda yet, the new Prelude.

One initiative of R&D was a six-stroke engine which aimed to reduce contamination of the incoming charge by the unburnt remnants of the exhaust gases in the combustion chamber. A small post-combustion passage regulated by an electrically-triggered valve burned the residue fuel during an extra stroke

of the piston. It was never put into production, but it exemplified the new spirit of enterprise among the researchers.

Engineers could now select their own study themes and once they gained approval took complete responsibility for a project. Fujisawa described the structure as "paperweight", in which project teams were on an equal footing with one another, as opposed to the customary "pyramid", a hierarchical system where engine and transmission initiatives took precedence over chassis design or styling. The objective was to smooth the path of design and development as a co-operative rather than a contentious procedure.

When Kiyoshi Kawashima took over the presidency in October 1973, Honda entered a new phase during which the company's growth was spectacular. In 1973 its turnover was scarcely 400 billion yen, yet in 1979 it exceeded 1 trillion yen and by 1980 was 1.5 trillion yen. In barely 32 years it had achieved a tenth of the turnover of General Motors and was one-third the size of Toyota or Nissan. Honda was the first Japanese manufacturer set up after the war to reach the trillion yen benchmark, and although Fujisawa thought it should have If

1976. The first Accord (below left)

1980. The mature Accord had a CVCC II engine and optional semi-automatic 3-speed gearbox with overdrive (below)

ACCORD
The Accord was the first production car to appear under the SED (Sales Engineering and Development) procedure for inaugurating new models. A project team from each discipline studied what the customers wanted, developed a suitable product, and put it into production. The first Accord, launched in 1976, was aimed at older and more affluent buyers than the Civic and, although bigger, it followed Honda's cautious approach by inheriting not only the Civic's front-engine and front-wheel drive but some of its hardware as well. Yet its enduring attribute was

exemplary quality. The Accord reinforced Honda's reputation as one of the most satisfactory cars in the world to own. It was commended by the press for its dynamic qualities, quietness and refinement, goodmanners, and safe handling. Yet it was through its sheer competence in different ways that it gained the essential word-of-mouth endorsement from owners that inspired its extraordinary authority.

The first-generation Accord was a three-door, four-seat hatchback and a four-door saloon with a boot. It had 1,599cc or 1,602cc overhead camshaft engines, and either a five-speed gearbox of

praiseworthy smoothness or a two-speed Hondamatic. It was finely detailed inside, had independent suspension by coil springs and, although the styling was scarcely adventurous, it was well-proportioned and carried over a family resemblance from the Civic. Among the best aspects of its refinement were supple springing and light, precise steering.

Production of the first Accords lasted until 1983, with a total of 1,170,712 made until it was replaced by the Accord DX and EX, an interim model built until 1985. The eight-valve 1,602cc engine was supplemented by a 12-valve 1,829cc 100bhp unit in 1984, the car was made larger to provide more room inside and the top models gained air conditioning and cruise control.

attained it earlier, it represented a significant accomplishment. Kawashima inherited a new management structure which replaced the original open-plan office arrangement Fujisawa put in place in the fledgling years of the 1950s.

The management changeover also coincided with the first world oil crisis which brought inflation and recession to Japan. It coincided too with new emission control proposals which reverberated through the R&D departments of car manufacturers round the world. Prices of cars and motorcycles rose by 7-8 per cent followed by a further 10 per cent in the autumn of 1973. Every manufacturer except Honda raised prices; Honda was already well ahead in meeting exhaust legislation and was adopting a new strategy of expansion to keep unit costs down through an increase in car and truck production to a million units a year. Motorcycle production went up to 3 million, 1 million made and sold in Japan, a further million made in Japan and sold abroad, and a million now made outside Japan. Finally Kawashima embarked on an expansion of Honda's power products, which included generators, tillers, lawn mowers, outboard motors, and water pumps, in Honda's best tradition of making compact high performance engines.

A key element in Honda's expansionist strategy was the development of the American Honda Motor Company Inc., with plans for a car plant at Marysville. The company was set up in 1959, the first of Honda's overseas subsidiaries, closely followed by European Honda GmbH (later Honda Deutschland) in Hamburg in 1961, and NV Honda Motor SA (later Honda Belgium). Honda Benelux began operations in 1963 and in 1964 Honda France SA was established in Paris with an office close by the famous Crazy Horse Saloon – "in order to blend with the culture", it was claimed – and Asian Honda began operations in Thailand.

In September 1965 Honda UK was set up in Power Road, Chiswick, west London, followed by developments in Australia and Canada, so by the time Honda exported its 12 millionth motorcycle in August 1969, it was essentially a world company.

The overseas companies were a diverse lot. Some were importers, a few assembled motorcycles, but an American factory making Hondas was a new departure. It was first contemplated in 1971, the year motorcycle production reached 15 million units, and a project team was set up in 1975 to select the site and begin construction. In 1977 the plans for motorcycle production were announced with the Honda of America Manufacturing Company, a joint venture between Honda Motor and American Honda Inc. Honda Europe NV was set up in Gent, Belgium, to buy components and co-ordinate the supply of new cars. Motorcycle production in 1978 topped the 30 million mark and cars reached 5 million.

It was 1979 before the first Honda motorcycle was made in Ohio and a year later before plans for the car plant were made public. A significant part of the rationale for local manufacture was the protectionist stance taken both in America and Europe against imports from throughout the Pacific rim

Engineers' dream a success. Steering control of four wheels gave Prelude new stability and controlled yaw (below right)

Plain mechanical linkage of the first four wheel steering was elegant engineering. Rear wheels steered with the fronts for the first one-third turn of the steering wheel, then counter-steered 5.3 degrees (far right)

PRELUDE

Car manufacturing economics depend heavily on volume, and getting the most out of the Accord's underpinnings included introducing a separate model on them. This was the Prelude, a two-door coupe with less space than the saloon, which, in the way of things, cost more. The first Prelude with the Accord's 1.6-litre engine and front-drive transmission looked a little severe. It was equipped with the **CVCC** engine in 1980, and the **XXR** was added in 1981

swerving or cornering. Many doubted the value of steering the extra set of wheels but Honda's approach, with a mechanical system that displayed ingenuity rather than electro-hydraulic complication, was reassuringly simple.

Soon every Japanese manufacturer had four-wheel steering either in production or under development, and others such as Porsche incorporated rear suspension arrangements that included a measure of rear wheel steer. Honda managed what

satisfactory behaviour on the road was not a question of tyre-wrenching grip and traction, so much as precision and sensitivity. It also replaced the pioneering mechanical four-wheel steering with a sophisticated electronic system. Designed in Honda's Californian styling studio, and aimed at America with Europe in mind, it was a tougher, more robust looking car than its predecessor and competed with more obviously sporting competitors from Toyota and Nissan.

but it was not until a new rebodied **Prelude** appeared towards the end of 1982 that the model achieved the success it deserved.

Pop-up headlamps, clean lines, and a 1.8-litre 12-valve engine giving 103bhp and a relatively modest 103mph was scarcely exciting but the Prelude somehow symbolised Honda's quiet progress towards fast, cultured, discreet-looking cars. This was the vehicle that was used to introduce a pioneering technology that astonished the motoring world in 1986 – four-wheel steering.

The best tribute to four-wheel steering was that it was possible to drive a Prelude quite a long way without noticing it, but a driver would be insensitive not to observe the responsiveness and absence of body-roll when

engineers from the dawn of motoring, including the British racing driver Freddie Dixon in the 1930s, had been trying for, namely to control and drive each wheel indepenently.

The **Prelude** of 1991 had a new Oriental grace and further enhanced its growing reputation for good handling. It took cues from the **NSX** by demonstrating that

countries. But while the American answer was to build
a transplant factory, in Europe the solution was rather different.

The pact between Rover and Honda was important to both
companies and even though it decayed following BMW's
takeover of Rover in 1994, it endured well into the second half
of the 1990s in the tangible form of a joint model policy on the
lines conceived by Sir Michael Edwardes and Kiyoshi Kawashima
in December 1979. It began with a licence-built Honda Ballade
and developed with co-operative models leading to a mutual
stakeholding in the 1990s under which Honda owned 20 per
cent of Rover, and Rover 20 per cent of Honda's UK
manufacturing affiliate. For Rover it meant rehabilitation after
years of despondency, crippling labour disputes, and falling sales.
For Honda it was a window on Europe, an opportunity to
circumvent the protectionism that put up trade barriers in some
European markets, notably France and Italy.

The first phase was a low-key, "programme of collaboration",
that developed into a working relationship with the British-built
Ballade launched in September 1980 as the Triumph Acclaim.
Essentially a booted derivative of the 1970s hatchback Civic, the
Ballade had front-wheel drive, a 1.3-litre four-cylinder transverse
engine with 70bhp, an overhead camshaft, and a silky five-speed
gearbox. The body styling was hardly up-to-the-minute but, like
most Hondas, it had evolved coherently rather than having been
subjected to "designer" facelifts. The rectangular headlamps, the
wide stance for a medium-sized saloon and fine detailing were
to be significant in the history of the European motor industry.
The precision of Honda's body-tooling made the door shut-lines
narrow; it was a car of good quality at a price for which many
European cars were still badly made.

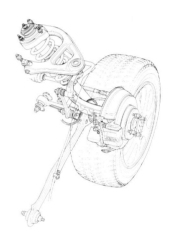

By the 1990s
Preludes were
faster, stylish,
racy (right)

Rear (far right).
Electronic four
wheel steer,
disc brake and
drum for
handbrake,
double
wishbone
suspension.

Ride-on
mowing (left
and below left).
In an English
country garden,
the Honda
3009

Hondas at
home.
Appropriate
cherished
number for the
CRX, a sporty
Civic (left)

Child's play
(below)

MOWERS

Honda suffered no sense
of irony in making lawn
mowers for the world even
though in Japan's crowded
islands not many homes had
lawns, let alone mowers.

Honda supplied engines,
industrial power packs in
effect, for a variety of uses
throughout its history, for
agricultural machines, pumps,
generators, construction
equipment, welding plant,
and even (for a time) rival
motorcycles.

Development of its own
products was logical and in due
course included such diverse
equipment as mini-combine
harvesters and caterpillar-
tracked wheelbarrows.

Lawn mowing machinery
came in two sorts – those
pushed or controlled by
someone on foot, and those on
which the operator rode.

Yet even though engines
were the cornerstone of all
Honda's activities, just like
motorcycles or cars, lawn
mowers were designed from
the ground up as lawn mowers.
They were not simply
platforms for an engine, they
were conceived as grass-
cutters, an engineering

challenge seemingly taken
up as ardently as winning
the Isle of Man TT.

Honda developed its own
hydrostatic transmission which
produced drive from moving
oil like a car's automatic
transmission, rather than sets
of gears. Annular oil-filled
pistons rotated by a circular
plate drove a motor by
hydraulic pressure to provide
a smooth and infinitely
variable drive. Riding mowers
had four-stroke engines air-
cooled or liquid-cooled, a
choice of manual or
hydrostatic transmission, a
stout steel chassis, and rack-
and-pinion steering.

Triumph
Acclaim, 1981
(below).
Honda Ballade
the best quality
built in Britain
for years

Public interest in the Acclaim was intense. The UK government had invested heavily in British Leyland, creating a plant to build the Metro for a company that was effectively the rump of the entire old British motor industry. It was also a focus of the protectionist measures that gave rise to a gentlemanly quota arrangement between the British Society of Motor Manufacturers and Traders (SMMT) and the Japanese Automobile Manufacturers' Association (JAMA) intended to take the heat out of the dispute over the level of Japanese imports. A near-moribund Rover seemed an unlikely partner for vigorous and expanding Honda, yet, as with the licensing agreements for the CVCC engine technology in the 1970s, co-operation of this sort was expedient and made good business sense.

The Triumph Acclaim launched at Motorfair, Earls Court, London, in October 1981 struck a chord at once. Its build quality by the standards of the British motor industry of the time was exemplary, establishing a number of important issues not only for the domestic audience, but for European cars in general. The significance of the Acclaim was to show that high-quality production was possible in a European factory – not a greenfield transplant like that proposed for Marysville, but one deep in the heart of the old smokestack motor industry. It showed European customers that Japanese quality was not a trick of the light, but a standard that all cars should reach.

Civic pride.
(overleaf)
Evolutionary
development
brought new
levels of
refinement
to family car
market

If old British Leyland could make a car from which pieces did not fall, and which could provide reliable service, customers would no longer put up with anything less. The launch of the Acclaim was as significant as the arrival of the first Honda motorcycles in the 1960s. The difference this time was that unlike the Norton, AJS, Triumph, and BSA managements that were passing into history, the indigenous enterprises paid attention. The principal beneficiaries were European consumers who now demanded that all cars should be as reliable as the Acclaim. Its influence was immediate and enduring.

The Acclaim was made with 80 per cent British parts although the engine, transmission, and some of the difficult facia mouldings were brought in from Japan. About £70 million was invested at British Leyland's plant at Cowley, near Oxford, installing new robotic welding equipment. The first 200 pre-production Acclaims were off the line by mid-March, 1981. By July, production was in full swing and by the official announcement to the press in September, 6,000 cars were ready for the road. It was a telling contrast to many bungled Leyland launches when only a handful of cars would be ready, and customers had to carry out the shake-down tests.

Honda's sports car and racing heritage, its splendid motorcycles and reputation for superb engineering gave the

Compact, portable, lightweight. self-contained generators (below) provided heat and light remote from power supplies

GENERATORS

Honda started with small, simple, two-stroke proprietary engines left over from the war, with which it turned pedal cycles into primitive motorcycles. It soon began making its own engines and in 1953, six years after the company was formed, started selling them to power other firms' products, mostly pumps or agricultural machinery. Honda carried on selling engines well into the 1990s, and they were employed for use in everything from road-making implements, such as vibrating compactors, to blowers for inflating hot-air balloons.

By the 1960s, generating electrical power was a key activity for industry and there was also a growing leisure market requiring portable power far from mains electricity. Following the success of the general purpose engines that Honda began selling in 1953, it was logical to introduce a complete portable generator of its own; the E300 came in January 1965.

At first all a generator had to do was generate, then it had to weigh less, run longer, control its exhaust emissions, regulate its own voltage, let its operator know if it was low on oil, pump its own fuel, and make less noise. The more expensive ones also had to start on a button rather than with a pull on a rope.

Once again the secret lay in Honda's engines; soon they were all four-stroke, later all overhead valve and all made, like the motorcycle engines, from aluminium die-castings so carefully machined that they could often be assembled without gaskets and still not leak oil.

The small handy generators kept lights burning on campsites without disturbing the peace, and were no noisier than someone talking a metre away.

Of all Honda's power products, the larger generators had some of their most elegant engines, with automatic decompression for easy starting and steel cylinder liners. They included V-twins and vertical twins, liquid-cooled and air-cooled, and one of Honda's few production diesels.

Swindon
Accord.
Sideways
moves on
production line
made the
Swindon
factory
compact
(below)

Acclaim a vigorous start. The customers felt that Rover was dealing once again with engineers, practical people, not accountants or trade unionists of whom they had grown weary. The Acclaim was more luxurious than the Ballade and although not fast or smooth-riding, it was a striking success. There was a brisk market among clients not interested in speed, who mostly drove on smooth roads, rarely carried more than two people and above all craved reliability.

For them it was quiet, well-proportioned and well-equipped, and was offered with Honda's exquisitely engineered miniature air conditioning unit, an unheard-of luxury for a 1.3-litre car. Rather disappointingly, when Rover reasserted its own brand-name and called its next Ballade the Rover 200, there was still not enough room in the back, the ride was uneven and it had a high sill to the luggage boot.

Faults like these represented a temporary aberration yet it remained dependable, the finish was luxurious for a middle-sized car, and it seemed almost a match for a small BMW in quality if not in speed or handling, even if it was not much cheaper. The ride was later tranquillised and the boot redesigned to assuage its shortcomings, but the essential quality was maintained and Rover recovered its place in the market faster than anybody dared hope thanks largely to the stimulus from Honda. Fastidious private owners liked the rich equipment, deep upholstery, and well-finished interior of the Rover Vanden Plas. For Honda the partnership not only provided a window on Europe, it also gave an insight into European tastes in marketing and furnishings.

The Honda H grew taller over the years. Compare the modern version (left) with the wider version on a 1960s S800 (below)

HONDA UK

From 1961 until Honda UK Ltd was set up officially in London in September 1965, sales, stores, spares and imports were being handled from a former Raleigh Bicycles warehouse in Nottingham. Jim Harrisson's firm Hondas Ltd imported the first motorcycles to small premises in Soho, and at the Earls Court Cycle and Motorcycle Show in November 1962, exhibited a 170cc four-stroke Juno M85 scooter with a horizontally-opposed twin cylinder engine ahead of the rider's feet and a Badalini hydraulic automatic transmission.

A subsidiary of Honda Motor in Tokyo, Honda UK was established with capital of £267,957 and 119 employees. It moved into the appropriately-named Power Road, Chiswick, west London, to a brick-faced office block with a workshop on the ground floor so evocative of post-war commercial buildings that by the 1990s it was listed for preservation. Honda UK's

subsidiaries were European Honda Motor Trading GmbH in Hamburg, and its affiliates, European Honda SA and Honda France.

The motorcycle workshop facilities and spares for power products remained at Nottingham, and the first car, the S800 was shown at the Earls Court motor show, London, in 1966. It took six weeks to bring the cars from Tokyo to the docks of London, a thriving port in the 1960s.

They arrived on Ben Line and Glen Line cargo ships before purpose-built car-carrying vessels came into general service. They were steam-cleaned and prepared for dispatch at the shipper's depot in the East End of London before being sent out to dealers, of which there were still only 45 in 1967.

A service training school was set up in Chiswick, the first S800 racing car for Tetsu Ikusawa was prepared there,

and there were three Japanese directors, Mukoyama, the managing director, Tetsu Chino the marketing director, and Saida, the company secretary. Jim Harrisson was Honda's sales manager and the publicity manager was David Palmer.

The 1967 sterling crisis, in which the Wilson government devalued the pound by 14.3 per cent, was weathered successfully, the annual report concluding that, "UK sterling has been translated at the new rate of £1 = US$ 2.40. The effect of the devaluation ... is not significant". But Honda France and Honda Motor SA were nevertheless made independent of the UK. In April 1991 Honda UK (HUK) under Toshio Ishino became a division of Honda Motor Europe Ltd (HME), set up with headquarters in Reading to co-ordinate all the European subsidiaries. Its president, Kazue Ito, became chief operating executive for the Middle East and Africa.

The co-operative programme known as Project XX began in earnest in 1986 with the Rover 800, and continued into the 1990s with the second generation 200 and 400, the joint Concerto programme, and the Rover 600/Honda Accord. The mechanically similar cars were made at Longbridge, Birmingham, but it soon became evident that Honda's expansion warranted a factory of its own, first for engines and pre-delivery checks to bring Rover-made Hondas up to scratch, and in due course for new Accords and the Civic 5-door.

The Concerto's controls were light, the seats comfortable, the styling clean and well-proportioned, but the ride remained capricious. While it was even and level on most roads, the car heaved on large bumps. Safe, relaxed, and with few sporty pretensions, the Concerto could be driven enjoyably quickly.

In June 1986, the launch of the Rover 800 and Honda Legend marked a new phase in the Rover-Honda relationship.

Joint product. Honda Concerto (above), distinctive hatchback of 1990

Rover luxury.
British-designed
and executed
interiors were
among the best
of their kind, as
in the Rover
Sterling (right)

The square-
rigged Rover
213 of 1987
(below)

The Fastback
Vitesse had no
Honda
equivalent in
1988 (below
right)

ROVER

Honda's relationship with Rover exemplified the measured approach of Japanese business diplomacy, yet it was the aggressive stance of Continental European car manufacturing that eventually brought about its decay.

After BMW took control of Rover the affiliation that brought benefits to both sides had to change, and although Rovers and Hondas continued to cross-reference well into the second half of the 1990s, the old-style co-operation that began with the Triumph Acclaim was at an end.

The foresight shown by Sir Michael Edwardes and Kiyoshi Kawashima in forging the original link marked a profound change in post-war British industrial culture.

Quality improved, and a lasting change took place in workplace relations. The evolutionary procedure that brought this about may have been reminiscent of Rover in the 1930s although it was scarcely characteristic of the short-term policies of Austin, Morris, the British Motor Corporation, and later British Leyland. The arrangement had its critics within Honda, and even Kawamoto was incautious enough to remark at the 1988 Detroit Grand Prix that Honda did not seem to be getting much out of it.

Kume said: "Our objective from the start was to engage in projects where we might find mutual benefit while keeping our separate identities. There was never a grand strategy or plan. Each step was taken on its merits and we never quite saw Austin Rover as a Honda factory in Britain. While it gave Honda access to assembly facilities in Britain, that was not all there was to it. Building cars in Britain with a local content gave us access to the European market, but that was not our sole strategy for Europe. We saw the possibility of shipping cars from America."

Any prospect of Honda taking over Rover's mainstream car development disappeared when BMW took over in 1994. Co-operation continued in body production, and Honda used Rover diesel engines, but reciprocal model development ceased.

Businesslike
facia of 1988
Legend
(far right)

Coupe lines
echoed the
Prelude.
(below)

Conceived and developed in a joint cross-world programme
rather than simply made under licence like the Triumph Acclaim,
the 800 replaced the 10-year-old SD1. Tadashi Kume said
guardedly at the launch that despite occasions "where no
resolution could be reached" the co-operation had been "truly
satisfying". It was not long before the Legend moved ahead,
relinquishing the Rover ingredients, and by 1989 it was bigger
and acquired a 3-litre V-6 power unit with variable valve timing.
The flared wings and some of the embellishments went, and the
resulting car was the better for it.

Rover remained Honda's European foothold until its
manufacturing facility at South Marston near Swindon came into
production. By the early 1990s the first of three joint ventures,
code-named Synchro, were produced in Swindon. The Honda
versions replaced a number of Japanese-built imports and the
Rovers were styled with traditional Rover features including
a neat grille corresponding with the radiator shell of Rovers
of the 1930s.

Rear loading area made the most of Civic's wheelbase (above, top)

The 1973 Civic, with strut suspension front and rear, and a CVCC engine (above)

Larger Civic: the 1500 3DCX of 1979 with 80bhp (SAE) 64bhp (net) 70bhp (DIN) (above right)

CIVIC

Honda secured its place among the leading car makers of the world in July 1972 with the first Civic, a front-wheel drive transverse engined 1.2-litre hatchback that formed a basic platform for the remainder of the 1970s. The first Civic had 54bhp, and was followed for Japan and the United States with the 60bhp 1,169cc CVCC stratified charge engine with its three-valve head. Europe had an older engine with up to 72bhp, followed by a 1,488cc version introduced in 1973.

Honda – never a modest company – hoped the Civic would have the same impact on the US market as the Volkswagen Beetle had in the 1960s. Soichiro Honda

even wanted to make it air-cooled as the Beetle was. Like the VW, it had independent suspension but by struts front and rear rather than the VW's trailing arms and swing-axles. An unpretentious small economy car, it soon began a process of progressive enlargement and enhancement which continued throughout its life. At first it made a relatively minor impression in Europe, partly because it was small and partly because, like many Japanese cars of the time brought to a damp climate, it grew rusty.

Honda learned its lesson, and in the 1980s better-class, rust-free Civics proliferated. By the restyle of 1983, although it was still sold in the UK only as a hatchback with the Triumph Acclaim accounting for the Ballade market, build quality reached the standards for which Honda became famous. Ride quality was still firm by European ideals, but bigger and better engines – from 1987 incorporating VTEC technology - made the Civic

lively yet economical. All the engines had 16 valves, two of the 1.6-litre units had twin overhead camshafts, and body variants included the tall estate-car style called the Shuttle, available with four-wheel drive, and the sporty CRX.

The CRX had the Civic's 93in wheelbase and a 3-door fastback coupe body. The 1984 edition had 100bhp, and the 1986 1.6i 150bhp giving the little car a fierce performance, achieving 0-60mph in 7.5sec, and a top speed of close on 130mph.

By the dawn of the 1990s nimble and relatively slow sports cars were more acceptable than large fast ones, and even keen drivers came to regard owning a Ferrari as about as sensible as owning a steam locomotive – agreeable if cash was abundant and it was to be admired or run on a private track, but otherwise something of a burden.

Yet a Honda CRX was as enjoyable at 60mph on the road as an NSX at 160mph. The distinction lay in practicality, and although speed was an ingredient in the enjoyment of both, cornering the CRX at 60mph could be as absorbing as the NSX at twice the speed.

If the CRX looked unprepossessing, the engine was memorable. At low speeds it behaved as politely as any mid-sized four-cylinder, pulling strongly and evenly. At high speeds the VTEC variable cam mechanism came into play, transforming it into a high-revving sports engine spinning smoothly to 7,600 rpm for the 158 horse power available by the 1990s. It revved shrilly to the red line on the rev counter at 8,000rpm.

The CRX convertible had an aluminium roof panel to provide open-air motoring with more security than a folding hood. It stowed underneath the boot lid, imposing a limit on how high suitcases could be piled, but there was sufficient space for holiday luggage for two.

CRX, Honda's claim to the youth market (below). Best Honda sports car since the S800

CRX facia (right). Few concessions to luxury, but efficient and well-proportioned

Horse power
replaced by
horsepower.
Honda engines
harnessed for
agriculture
(right)

Potato cropping
made easy
(below)

TILLERS

Honda's first agricultural
engine was the H-type in 1953,
a two-stroke adapted from
a motorcycle engine, used
mostly as a water-pump and
followed by a number of
general purpose engines
put to various uses by
manufacturers of power
equipment. Honda's first
power tiller, the F150, went
on sale in 1959, followed by
the more powerful F190
in 1961.

Only the smallest and
cheapest continued with
a two-stroke engine,
a 34cc 1hp, and weighed
an easily-portable 15.3kg
(33.6lb). The rest of the range,
which grew more powerful
and more easily handled over
the years, had four-stroke
engines – the small ones with

side valves, larger ones up
to 8hp with overhead valves.
By 1980 a million had been
made towards Honda's 1992
total of 20 million units of
power products.

The Jazz with CVCC engine (far right), 45bhp for economy, 110bhp with turbo and intercooler. Pininfarina made a sports version.

Honda consistently won approval by consumers in America and Europe. In 1986 it was rated number one in the important J D Power US customer satisfaction index, which measured not just the quality and reliability of cars but the success of dealers in sustaining their reputation by providing good service. Magazines, including *Car and Driver* in the United States, *Autocar, What Car?* and many others in Europe, heaped praise and awards on Honda. Japanese models dominated lists of the most reliable cars on British roads published by the Consumers' Association's *Which?* magazine in Britain, Rover crucially winning a high placing in the table with its 213, manufactured at Longbridge. It would never have gained such an endorsement in the pre-Honda era.

Production at Honda of America began in November 1982 with the first US-built Accord and developed to be the most extensive of any Japanese manufacturer, with the Accord becoming America's best selling car. Honda's sales outstripped those in Japan and its huge investment in the United States, mostly locally generated, gave rise to speculation that Honda was almost more American than Japanese. "America is one of our most important markets and we want to achieve substantial autonomy for our American operations, which is why we have invested heavily in research and development facilities. Our engineering subsidiary that produces our manufacturing equipment has also invested in the US, but that doesn't mean we are about to uproot. We shall stay in Japan. If any evolution takes place it will be not towards being either an American company or a Japanese company but towards being a true multinational," said Kume.

The most far-reaching American development was setting up the Acura division, giving the up-market cars a brand-name and a cachet that triggered rival bids for the hearts and minds of wealthy Americans by Nissan, with Infiniti, and Toyota, with Lexus. In the end the newcomers rather upstaged the Acura which turned out not to be up-market enough and suffered from rather plain styling.

When Nobuhiko Kawamoto took over the reins in June 1990 his credentials were impeccable. At 54 he was outspoken, but after years spent with the racing programme, then as head of R&D he had something to be outspoken about. His first task was to rekindle Honda's home market. Honda was doing well in America and making headway in Europe but did not have a network on its home ground to fend off Nissan and Toyota, particularly at the top end of the domestic market where it seemed to lack the marketing proficiency to sell the Legend.

Under Kawamoto it was a matter of time before Honda would concede the autonomy of its transplant enterprises to include not only local component procurement and market research, but also a commitment to design, engineer, and style cars in its overseas markets. Kawamoto, perhaps the most international of all Honda's presidents, recognised that there were subtle features in Europe or the United States that a manufacturer had to address. "Fiat makes particularly Italian

The former Vickers-Supermarine site at South Marston, near Swindon developed for Honda manufacture (right). Wartime Spitfires took off from runways that now form the car test track

Accord on the line (below)

SWINDON

Honda's 1987 annual report announced that following the success of the Triumph Acclaim, the Rover-badged Honda Ballades, the Rover 800/Honda Legend and the Rover 400/Honda Concerto, it would sign an agreement with BL, the Austin Rover Group, to produce another joint car to go on sale through each other's dealers. The European Accord would be jointly developed, and made by Rover using engines built at a new Honda plant due to be completed at Swindon, England, in 1989. Its capacity was to be 70,000 engines a year.

Full car production, whatever Honda maintained, was always an option for Swindon, and in July 1989 Honda UK Manufacturing (HUM) announced plans for an extension to be finished by the end of 1992, to build 100,000 cars a year. Rover and HUM formally completed the deal in April 1990 which gave Rover a 20 per cent holding in Honda UK Manufacturing (HUM), while Honda took 20 per cent of Rover's shares and paid £30 million in cash to bring the value of the share exchanges to the same level. Each company had a non-executive director on the other's board. Soichiro Irimajiri, a senior managing director, joined Rover and John Towers, then product development director of Rover, sat on the HUM board. The cars jointly built in Britain were aimed at the single European market expected to open up in the 1990s.

Right on schedule, a ceremony in October 1992 celebrated the beginning of production at Swindon of the Accord, made in tandem with the Rover 600 at Cowley, Oxford.

Swindon's car production was expected to reach 100,000 by the middle of the decade. The cars had body panels produced by Rover at Longbridge, Birmingham, and while most engines and gearboxes came from Honda at Swindon some Rovers had engines and transmissions produced at Longbridge.

By 1995 following production of its 100,000th car, Swindon was making arrangements for a 50 per cent expansion from 100,000 to 150,000 units per year.

The Aerodeck
Accord from
Marysville
(below)

cars, Citroën and Peugeot French cars. After the unification
of Europe, cars will become more international and we shall
have to consider making a Europeanised car," he said soon
after taking over.

In America autonomy meant a Californian design facility with
three luxurious studios in Torrance (one for cars, one for
motorcycles, one for power equipment) run by Charles Allen.
"This is an outdoors society," he told *Car* magazine in 1991.
"Boat engines, jet skis, lawn mowers, and generators are big
business here." Honda California designed several notable cars,
including the 1982 and 1986 Accord hatchbacks, the 1988 Civic
and the 1991 Accord Coupe. The CRX was initiated in
California as well as the long roof design for the Civic hatchback,
but the Accord, America's best-selling car, was designed in Japan.

Smooth
contours of
the 1990
Accord
(below)

Belt drive twin-
cam transverse
engine,
characteristically
Honda (below
right)

ACCORD

The 1985 Accords moved up-market. They had 2-litre engines, the single-cam 12-valve version giving 106bhp with carburettors and 122bhp with fuel injection, and the twin-cam 16-valve 2.0i-16, 137bhp. The handling did not quite keep pace with the engine engineering – a persistent niggle in both cars and motorcycles in the 1970s and 1980s – although the suspension developed from the struts of earlier Accords to Honda's estimable but costly wishbones. The strategy of making few compromises

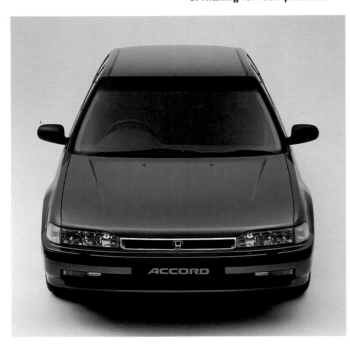

in engineering bore fruit in agreeable owner-satisfaction surveys.

The four-door, five-seat saloon had a top speed of 114mph and 0-60 acceleration inside the benchmark 10.0sec. The Aerodeck, Honda's name for a sort of estate car that was really something nearer a hatchback, had niggardly load space and was scarcely fast enough to be a sports estate like the Lancia HPE.

The hatchback, dropped in 1985, was replaced by the Integra a year later. This had front-end styling borrowed from the Aerodeck and a fastback sloping rear giving it,

too, an air of uncertainty about its role. Still, it filled a gap in the market and like all Accords was commercially a huge success. Each version sold well over a million.

The fourth generation of the Accord made between 1989 and 1992 was the last brought from Japan to Europe before production started at Swindon. Bigger, faster (132mph and 0-60 in 8.4sec) and better-equipped, like BMW and Mercedes-Benz and classic European makes, Honda followed an evolutionary approach so that although the car was entirely new, it could be parked alongside an older model and pass almost unnoticed.

It at last challenged European cars for ride and handling, increasing suspension travel by a useful 20 per cent. Only the ride let it down but the handling was approaching the best in the class. Just as the European programme was announced at the Frankfurt motor show, a new range of engines, including a five-cylinder, was launched in Japan. The grown-up European-market cars had new KG-series engines with two counter-rotating balancer shafts and fluid-filled mountings switching automatically into firm mode when the engine speed rose above an idle. The balancer shafts cancelled out internal vibrations and the fluid mountings reduced harshness in traffic.

Honda's policy of not compromising in engineering to get what it wanted – quietness and refinement – was a timely echo of the balancer shaft's inventor, the great Dr Frederick William Lanchester (1868-1946) whose studies of engine vibrations led to spinning shafts with counterweights that effaced an engine's out-of-balance forces. A 2.2-litre 150bhp

version was furnished with the four-wheel steering system from the pioneering Prelude, and when the estate car appeared it was a proper high-capacity affair made in America.

Honda UK was restricted to importing around 23,000 cars from Japan but it already imported American-made Honda motorcycles.

Bringing cars to Britain from America in 1991 was more than a tidy way of avoiding import quotas, for it also increased the range of Hondas available in Britain. So the Accord estate became the first Japanese-badged car built in the US and exported to Europe. About 2,000 were planned to come from Marysville in the first year. The Accord somehow symbolised the success of Japanese car manufacturers in America, where it became the best selling car in 1989 in a market where Japanese models took more than a third of sales.

Marysville worked overtime to increase annual capacity from 360,000 cars to more than 379,000 and planned to send 5,000 Accord estates a year to Europe. These were designed in America specifically for the United States but also to compete in Europe with key models such as Ford Sierra estates, Vauxhall Carlton estates and the Rover 800 hatchback.

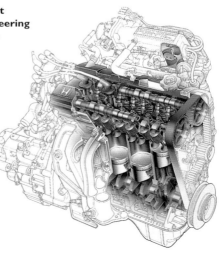

The exhaust-driven turbocharger on the left bank of cylinders of the winning 4-cam V-6 Williams-Honda at the Brazil Grand Prix of 1986 (left)

Honda's return to Formula One in the 1980s was more measured than its endeavours of the 1960s. It was determined to restore the reputation generated by Brabham's extraordinary run of success in Formula Two in the 1960s, and Ginther's last-gasp 1.5-litre win in 1965. The 3-litre experience, the air-cooled argument, Surtees's acerbic interlude, even Schlesser's death, had to be erased or at least acquitted before the old status quo could be re-established. The process began in the 1980s when the Bucknum card was played again in a low-key initiative leading to one of the most convincing demonstrations of racing engine superiority in the history of Formula One. A convincing win first time out with a new engine such as Jim Clark and the Lotus Ford-Cosworth 49 achieved in 1967 was out of the question – Formula One engine design was much too sophisticated for that in the 1980s – but what Honda did in the next 10 years was just as convincing.

Paul Frère, the distinguished Belgian journalist and Le Mans winner (1960 with Olivier Gendebien in a Ferrari) wrote that for a long time one important market eluded Honda, "... the market of what in Europe we call the 'noble' makes where the image plays a greater role than the price, the equipment, or even the technical concept. Six consecutive victories of Honda engines in the Formula One Manufacturers World Championship with two different chassis manufacturers and against competition from Ferrari, Porsche, Ford, and Renault as well as under two different sets of technical regulations (1.5-litre turbocharged with limited fuel consumption and 3.5-litre atmospheric) established Honda as one of the world's great car manufacturers and a world leader in technical progress."

Keke Rosberg drives to the shops. On the way to victory in the Australian Grand Prix, 1985 (right)

Frère paid tribute to Honda's policy of moving its engineers from racing to production activities and back again, and commented how readily racing experience was reflected in its products. "Honda was the first manufacturer in the world to market a popular car with a fully detoxed engine developing over 100bhp per litre, and running reliably and durably at more than 8,000rpm. Six years supremacy in Formula One gained Honda the world's respect and a place among the 'noble' makes."

Honda won 23 grands prix, one drivers' world championship and two constructors' world championships with Williams between 1984 and 1987. Frank Williams said that Honda brought a new approach to Formula One which was the acceptance only of excellence and technical supremacy. "Honda's method of working was new, as was their approach to the many problems encountered on the way to winning in Formula One. Honda's engineers had a special structure of management and communication, a special attitude to success and were entirely unafraid of hard work."

Honda moved to McLaren from 1988 to 1992 and won 44 more grands prix and the constructors' and drivers' titles four years in a row, a run of success unprecedented in modern grand prix motor racing. Ron Dennis, managing director of McLaren International spoke about the dedication and technical brilliance of the Honda engineers and mechanics which even adversaries admired. Luca Montezemolo, president of Ferrari spoke of the similarities between Honda and Ferrari, both founded by extraordinary individuals who loved motor racing and were committed to technical innovation although, it has to be added, the differences spoke for themselves.

Ambitions of success in motor racing remained rooted in Honda's corporate culture long after the bruising experience of the 1960s and compelled the re-entry to Formula One in the 1980s to be carefully planned. Engine research for Formula Two started in 1978, and co-operation with Ron Tauranac's Ralt team in 1980. Tauranac, a taciturn Australian, had long experience in Formula One as chief designer at Brabham, with drivers' and constructors' world titles to his credit in 1966 and 1967. Ralt's first Honda engine had insufficient low-speed pulling power but in its second season it took Geoff Lees to the Formula Two championship in Europe and Satoru Nakajima to victory in Japan. Honda was also back in motorcycle sport, winning the 500cc motocross championship of the world three years in a row. In 1983 Jonathan Palmer won the European F2 Championship with Ralt-Honda again, and as with Brabham in 1965 the car overwhelmed the opposition, scoring 12 consecutive victories from the seventh race of the 1983 season to the sixth of 1984.

Preparations for Formula One began in earnest in 1982 with plans for a 3-litre non-turbo, and V-6 and V-10 turbo engines based on the Formula Two design just as the Fédération Internationale du Sport Automobile, (FISA, the sport's governing body) brought in new wing and aerodynamics rules for 1983.

Tentative step. British Grand Prix, 1983 (right) Stefan Johansson with the Spirit Honda at Silverstone where he qualified fourteenth (ahead of Lauda and Mansell) in a field of 26. The car lasted only five laps of the race before a fuel pump belt came off

These gave turbocharged 1.5-litre engines the edge over 3-litre non-turbos. In 1982 Honda won its first motorcycle grand prix since making its comeback and sold its 3 millionth Civic in 10 years. The following year, 1983, brought Honda back to grand prix motor racing. A turbocharged 1.5-litre Honda Spirit Formula One "test bed" was driven by Stefan Johansson at the British Grand Prix in a programme which extended to a further five grands prix for the slender-bodied flat-bottomed car. The results were modest, but the experience was invaluable and vindicated the decision never again to arrive in motor racing under-prepared.

Plans were already under way to provide the Williams team of Keke Rosberg and Jacques Laffite with engines for 1984. Construction of the new FW09 Williams-Honda under Patrick Head began in the summer of 1983 and progress was so swift that it was ready to race in the South African Grand Prix at the end of the season. Honda gave the go-ahead, the car handled well, but an engineering enigma remained. The engineers still found it impossible to turn up the boost pressure sufficiently to provide competitive power without compromising reliability.

Williams hall
of fame
(overleaf)

The team was satisfied with finishing fifth and the prospects for 1984 looked promising.

The V-6 engine was very different from the non-turbo Ford-Cosworth to which Rosberg and Laffite had been accustomed. Its turbocharged power came in with a rush and even though there was not enough of it, Rosberg described the throttle pedal as being like a light switch, "on" or "off". "Put your foot down halfway and there is nothing," he said. "Put it down an inch further and there's too much."

The new season failed to come up to expectations. The quandary over turbo boost against reliability persisted, and it proved difficult to get the handling right. It was not a satisfactory state of affairs despite the invention of advanced telemetry systems that relayed every detail of the engine's performance to the engineers in the pits. Rosberg finished second in the first race of the new season, but it was the ninth, the United States Grand Prix at Dallas, before the team was in a winning position again. Rosberg finished first ahead of a Ferrari, a Lotus-Renault, and Laffite in the second Williams. However it was a quirky race on a deteriorating track, even though it showed that once the reliability and handling problems were put right, the engine was capable of winning through against the formidable TAG-Porsche engines used by McLaren.

Engine development was separated from race operations so that each group of technicians operated independently. Teams of engineers could be assigned wherever they were needed, an arrangement Patrick Faure, head of Renault Sport, believed gave Honda an important advantage. "What is unique to Honda is that the Formula One team is central to the company itself. At Renault it is a matter for Renault Sport, a company within a company."

Jacques Laffite left Williams and was replaced by Nigel Mansell for 1985, and the engine underwent an extensive redesign. The cylinder bore was reduced and water circulation improved which effectively made each cylinder individually cooled. Cylinder head cooling was also enhanced, dual fuel injection brought in and, to cope with the demands of individual tracks, different turbo compressors were designed to suit each one. No detail was overlooked in the search for power and reliability, yet it was well into the season before the problems were resolved sufficiently for both team cars to complete the course of a race, let alone score more victories. Rosberg won in Detroit, followed by two good second places. Then, towards the end of the season, the car found form and Nigel Mansell won twice in a row. Rosberg rounded off 1985 by winning the final race in Australia showing at last that the engine was a match for anything in the world.

From then on Honda's grip on Formula One racing was secure. In 1986 the Williams drivers were Nelson Piquet and Nigel Mansell. Piquet won four races and Mansell five, losing the world championship to Alain Prost after a 180mph tyre failure in the last race of the season, 80 miles from what looked like a secure victory. He missed the title by two frustrating

Nigel Mansell (Williams-Honda) wins the European Grand Prix at Brands Hatch, 1985 (left)

points. This was the year in which Frank Williams was in a mid-season road accident that left him paralysed; it was a tribute to his management skills and the regime he had established that Williams-Honda still won the constructors' championship.

In 1987 Honda engines were used by two teams, Lotus and Williams, giving Ayrton Senna (Lotus) two of the victories which confirmed his status among the greatest drivers of his time. They provided Nelson Piquet (Williams) with his third world championship after seven second places and three victories – the German, Hungarian, and Italian grands prix. His car failed to finish only twice.

The twin problem of power and reliability was now regarded as solved and the 165-168E engines, the 1.5-litre 80 degree V-6 introduced in 1985, proved versatile enough to deal with changes in the regulations concerning fuel consumption. Its power output reached 1,010PS (996bhp) at 12,000rpm with a boost pressure of 4 bar. Once boost was reduced to 2.5 bar under prevailing regulations and fuel tank capacity limited to 150 litres, it produced 685PS (676bhp) at 12,500rpm.

The 1988 season saw Honda move to McLaren, buying itself

Winning Williams. Nose-cone number 5 of Nigel Mansell in 1986 (right)

Senna portrait
by Craig
Warwick
(right).
Senna on
the left with
Soichiro
Honda,
and rival Alain
Prost (below)

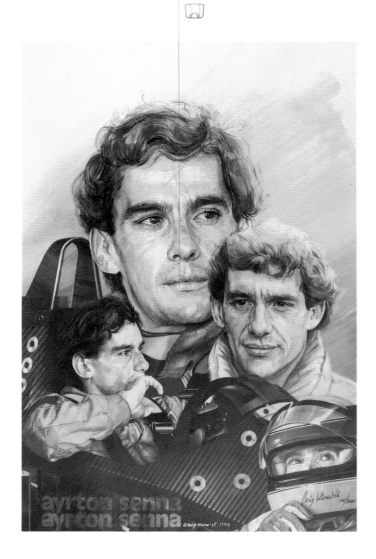

AYRTON SENNA

Ayrton Senna (1960-1994):
driver Lotus-Honda 1987;
McLaren Honda 1988-1992;
world champion McLaren-
Honda 1988, 1990, and 1991.

He contested 97 grands prix
with Honda engines, winning
32 of them, took pole position
33 times, and scored 14 fastest
laps.

Senna at Monza, September 1990, a characteristic performance. He was fastest in practice, set a new lap record, and led from lap 1 to lap 53 (right)

out of its Williams contract to achieve at last the motor racing ideal of providing the best drivers with the best engine, in the best car in the field. The results were conclusive. Ayrton Senna and Alain Prost in Marlboro McLaren Hondas won 15 out of 16 races (Senna eight to take the title, Prost seven), gained pole position 15 times out of 16 (Senna 13, Prost 2), finished first and second 10 times, and gained an unprecedented 199 points to win the constructors' cup.

Yet even during the frenzied activity that went with such a convincing display of superiority, three teams of engineers at the Tochigi research and development centre were looking into the 1988 regulations. These gave them the choice of a new 3.5-litre V-10, or continuing with the 2.5 bar-restricted 1.5-litre V-6 turbo. Their decision to stick with the turbo for one more season was vindicated, although work on the V-10 went on just the same. There was even a choice of turbo engines. The XE2 version provided superior economy, the XE3 better top-end pull, and they could be changed over as required to suit circuits where either fuel economy was vital or sheer power necessary.

Unfortunately in the course of the season, rivalry between the team drivers became acute. The French press was alarmed that Prost seemed to be getting less powerful engines than Senna – it looked like the only explanation for Senna showing such speed. The speculation became so intense that Jean-Marie Balaestre, the (French) president of the Fédération Internationale de l'Automobile (FIA) sent a formal letter to Tadashi Kume, demanding that he ensure both drivers had identical cars.

Honda was incredulous at the very idea and shrewdly published Kume's reply: "I believe that motor sports should

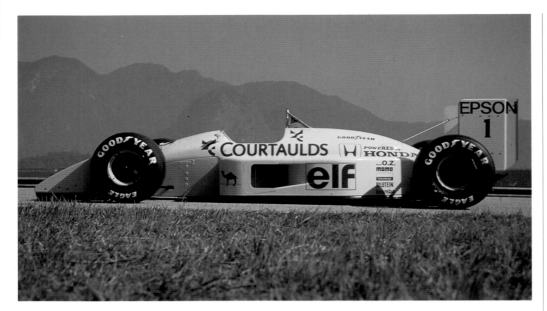

be conducted in a spirit of fair play and safety, in order to obtain the interest and emotional involvement of the spectators and people concerned. Honda Motor Co Ltd sees fairness as the highest requirement of its philosophy for conducting business and sets this quality as an ideology in its corporate dealings." Kume never heard complaints from Balaestre again. A Honda spokesman put it more simply at a press conference: "We would be quite prepared to line up four engines and let the drivers make their choice if that's what they would like."

Ron Dennis was more robust and demanded an apology from the FIA on discovering that Balaestre telephoned the Suzuka circuit during practice for the Japanese Grand Prix, commanding race officials to dismantle Prost's gearbox after the French driver complained of stiff gear selection. Dennis refused thereafter to have any technical inspections of his cars for anything other than the verification of race regulations.

In the end the results spoke for themselves as they did again in 1989 when the V-10 shown at the 1987 Tokyo motor show went into the back of a new McLaren. The turbo era ended in 1988 bringing in the 3.5-litre atmospheric engine. Ford and Ferrari went for new V-12s and Renault for a V-10. It was a measure of Honda's commitment to winning that its V-10 was race-ready by October 1988. The racing department was still determined never to be caught unprepared and the new unit was already fuel-efficient, powerful, and reliable after months of exhaustive testing at Suzuka by the McLaren test driver Emmanuele Pirro, who probably spent more time in the cockpit of a Formula One car that season than anybody, including the regular racing drivers.

By the Japanese Grand Prix of 1988, Renault's engine was only just installed in a car for the first time, Ferrari's was months behind schedule, Lamborghini's was not ready to be put in a car at all, and the Ford-Cosworth was scarcely past the design stage. By contrast Honda had eight RA109E engines ready for each of

Nelson Piquet's Camel Lotus-Honda, in 1988 livery for the British and German Grands Prix. (above)

Piquet (Williams-Honda), winner of 1986 Grand Prix of Brazil at Rio de Janeiro (left, top) and in the race (left, bottom)

Blazing
ambition.
World
champion
1988, Ayrton
Senna
(McLaren-
Honda) bids
farewell to
turbo-power
(below)

race, two for each race car and a spare plus two more for
emergencies. A late alteration in design, changing the camshaft
drive from belt to gears, involved close co-operation between
McLaren and Honda to incorporate the modification with
no more than a fortnight's delay to the test and development
schedule.

Such technical harmony was not echoed in the cockpits
of the racing cars. The belligerence between Prost and Senna
erupted early on when Prost accused his team-mate of breaking
a no-overtaking agreement in the rush for the first corner
at Imola. Senna, he claimed, was "not a man of honour". The two
scarcely spoke to one another again for the remainder of the
season, communicating through the engineers, testing the
stability of the McLaren-Honda relationship to its utmost.
Ron Dennis was torn between the extra turn of speed a certain
amount of rivalry can give a driver, and apprehension that the
two would be so busy racing one another that they might
overlook the real opposition.

Prost was reassured about the team's even-handed
preparation of his car by Osamu Goto, the engineering project
leader. It turned out to be true that there was a variation
between his and Senna's driving styles. The telemetry showed
that Senna used up more fuel because he worked the engine
harder, revved it higher, and made it produce more power for
longer. Prost was more sensitive and smoother, his light-footed
driving giving better fuel consumption which was particularly
important during the turbo era. The difference in power
between engines was never more than 5bhp however, a fine
tolerance which would have no effect on the track.

Prost was champion in 1989 and Senna runner-up, but not
before a controversial Japanese Grand Prix at Suzuka, home

NOBUHIKO KAWAMOTO

The president of Honda was once a racing mechanic for Jack Brabham. In the 1960s Nobuhiko Kawamoto worked in the competitive hothouse of an active and successful racing team following Honda's policy of grooming its top engineers and subsequently top executives by getting them to grips with engines early.

Kawamoto did not reach the highest position in Honda through the customary business channels of sales or accountancy. In engineering-led Honda, he designed and worked on many of the products that made it one of industry's technological leaders. He played a key role at Honda R&D from 1976 to 1989 and not only influenced production cars and motorcycles but also the successful Formula One racing programme. The **NSX** fulfilled a personal as well as a corporate ambition.

Kawamoto took over the job in June 1990 on the retirement of Tadashi Kume, with whom he had designed engines in the 1960s. When Honda pulled out of racing following Jo Schlesser's death in 1968, Kawamoto described the decision as "like an earthquake for the engineers". Honda needed to apply its R&D to solving the problems presented by the pending **US Clean Air Act**.

Though, by 1970, Kawamoto was chief engineer of Honda R&D, CVCC was really Tadashi Kume's idea.

Kawamoto proposed a smaller, high revving engine, with higher specific performance – a racing concept that he always cherished.

The first energy crisis of the 1970s was a challenging time for Honda, and Kawamoto said that one reason why the company was able to solve technical problems and adapt more quickly than the bigger manufacturers was "the spirit of initiative that the engineers had acquired in their contact with motor racing". In 1977, Kiyoshi Kawashima, who had been in charge of Honda's motorcycle racing team in the 1950s and had become president on Soichiro's retirement, declared that the time was right to re-enter racing.

Yet Kawamoto never lost sight of the rationale for racing – production car technology – and when turbos were forbidden in Formula One he, as an engineer, was disappointed. "We were getting close to 1bhp per cc at the end. Imagine what that could mean for a small production car – say, 60bhp from an engine so tiny you could hide it anywhere." He wanted smaller displacement engines in racing so that racing technology would be more directly applicable to road cars, and racing would be seen to be making a response to the environmentally-conscious 1990s.

Winning formula (left). Ayrton Senna, Nobuhiko Kawamoto, Gerhard Berger, Ron Dennis

Brabham mechanic, Formula Two engine plug change, 1966. Kawamoto's workmate in attendance with plug spanner (below)

Japan Grand
Prix, 1989,
lap 46. The
McLarens of
Senna and Prost
collide (right)

The 1988
MP4/4 with
turbocharger.
Engine RA168E,
V-6, 1,497cc,
11,800rpm,
675bhp with
84% toluene
and 16%
normal heptane
(below)

of Japanese motor racing and owned by Honda – although
it scarcely looked like it when the local enthusiasts erupted
in a display of Ferrari flags. The conflict that had been bubbling
up all season came to a head when Prost told Senna that he
was no longer going to give way if the Brazilian tried to
overtake. Several times during earlier races Senna had rushed
at corners and Prost backed off to avoid an accident. On lap 47
at Suzuka, with 10 to go, Prost led with Senna frantically setting
record laps in his efforts to make up for a bad start.   As the
pair reached   a tricky double bend Senna lunged forward;
Prost stood his ground and they collided.

There was a furious row. Stirling Moss said of Prost:
"He is one of the few drivers who display the same sort
of ethics that prevailed when I was driving." Prost, measured,
courteous and careful on the track, was seething. "I was certain
that I would win the race or have an accident like this," he said.
"Of course I realised that Senna absolutely wanted to win, but
his problem is that he can neither accept the possibility of not
winning, nor that somebody will resist his overtaking
manoeuvres. It has become absolutely impossible to work with
him." Dennis was not best pleased to have his team deprived
of victory and his cars damaged.

Senna tried to justify his position. "It was the only place
I could overtake," he said. "And somebody who should not have
been there just closed the door and that was that. The results
as they stand do not reflect the truth of the race in either the
sporting sense or in the sense of the regulations."   In the event
he was disqualified and his appeal for reinstatement rejected.

Prost left to join Ferrari for 1990, winning four races in a row
in the middle of the season to mount a strong challenge to
Senna for the world championship. The opposition had caught
up with the Honda V-10, pressed hard all season by the Ferrari
V-12 and sometimes by the Williams-Renault. The competition
was so keen that there were times when only Senna's brilliant
driving saved the day. The championship contest was close and
Senna once again blemished his reputation at the Japanese
Grand Prix in October, forcing Prost's Ferrari off the road on
the first lap apparently to ensure the world title would be his.
Jackie Stewart, a long-time campaigner for safe motor racing,
confronted Senna in a television interview, provoking an angry
defence of which Stewart said: "I think he
honestly believes what he is saying, but
then so did Hitler."

McLaren-Honda won the
constructors' championship
for the third year in a row,
a feat accomplished only
once before in the 33-year
history of the title.

Honda engines
powered the Marlboro
McLarens again in 1991,
and Honda also arranged

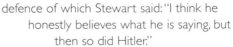

the Braun Tyrrells that Nakajima and Stefano Modena were to drive. They had an unhappy season, although it started well when the first of the Honda engines arrived in a crate at the team's headquarters at Ripley, Surrey. When Tyrrell technicians opened it, they found a V-10 engine wrapped in yellow ribbon with a card attached saying: "A Christmas present for the Tyrrell team from their new friends at Honda." It was a fine gesture which, alas counted for little when the engine was installed in a troublesome chassis.

McLaren changed to the new 121E V-12 which had been tested to destruction by Jonathan Palmer and Allan McNish. The new engine produced more power than the V-10 but it was still not enough for Senna, who pronounced himself dismayed at the start of the season. Akimasa Yasuoka, the new project manager, had to tell him it was detuned for reliability and Senna won the first four races just the same. Winning became more difficult as rivals found their feet, but at the Japanese Grand Prix in September, Gerhard Berger and Senna thrilled 250,000 Japanese with a dramatic 1-2 victory. Senna clinched the title, with Nigel Mansell second. The McLaren-Hondas won 8 races, the constructors' cup for a record sixth time and the drivers' championship for the fifth.

Yet the opposition was growing still stiffer. The V-10 Renault was a formidable competitor and easily beat off Ferrari and Ford. Patrick Faure saw Honda as the principal adversary. "We have frightened them, but not enough. We must do more," said the president of Renault Motor Sport, commercial head of the whole of Renault, and a crusader against what he regarded as the threat from the Japanese motor manufacturers. "We have three years to win the world championship. Two years ago I asked the man in charge of our F1 project, 'Can we beat the Japanese? Can we beat Honda?'."

Renault's choice of Williams was obvious: "The British are the best at running F1 teams, and of the two best, McLaren were already taken."

In 1992 Mansell won the first four races taking Williams-Renault to the constructors' cup two years ahead of Faure's aspirations, and winning at last his coveted and well-deserved drivers' title.

'Light as a V-8 with the power of a V-12', was Honda's promise to the McLaren designer for the start of the non-turbo era in 1989 (below)

Indycar Honda (left). First non-Cosworth, non-Ilmor engine to mount a credible challenge

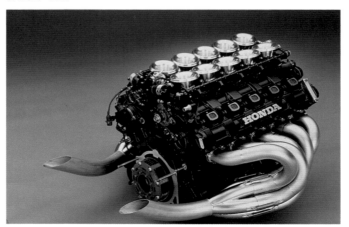

Trophy room,
McLaren
(above)

Honda and McLaren changed the engine shape to improve the car's aerodynamics, lowered its weight, introduced a semi-automatic transmission and put in active suspension, but, although Senna went on to win in Monaco, Hungary, and Italy, and Berger in Canada and Australia, the glory days were passing.

For any other team in motor racing, five grand prix victories in a season would have been outstanding. For McLaren, it was scarcely good enough. The car handled less than perfectly and the Honda V-12 was matched for power by newer rivals. Senna, so recently a world champion with Honda power, was ungracious about his prospects. He was not to know that even before the season began, Nobuhiko Kawamoto, president of Honda, had told Ron Dennis that Honda was likely to withdraw from Formula One at the end of 1992, and therefore he should consider options for the following season. "We wanted to consolidate our position. We confirmed our status in Europe as car makers through 10 years of competition and as a result we set up a factory and started sales channels throughout Europe. Accordingly, Formula One's role for us – to establish ourselves internationally as a major car maker – was finished."

With ATVs
Hadrian might
not have
needed a wall
(above).
Patrolling
would have
been easy

ALL TERRAIN VEHICLES

If aliens had invented a vehicle
for exploring the Earth they
would have come up with
something like an ATV.
The All-Terrain Cycle as it
was first known represented
ground-covering transport
at its basic best; a balloon-
tyred lunar rover for earthlings
not astronauts, it provided
mobility on unpredictable
terrain, could go where people
could not walk and, unlike off-
road vehicles of any other sort,
had a supple ride and was
cheap to run.

The serious side of the ATV
lay in its ability to carry, pull,
climb, spray, spread, and
scatter. It carried loads,
herded animals, and reached
outlying fields, prairies,
swamps or hills for the fence-
mender, linesman, vet,
explorer or rescuer. It was also

used for excursions nobody
wanted to make until the ATV
made them fun. It was
a vehicle that brought humans
the closest they ever came
to the classical Centaur
– a human head and torso
on the chassis of a horse.

The ATV owed its versatility
to squashy tyres inflated to
only 2.2psi giving it a soft
footprint, enabling it to cross
mud flats without sinking.
It would almost float on soft
slurry, gripping and driving
through all four of its deeply-
treaded chunky tyres. It could
bounce across a firmly-
ploughed field without the
rider/driver losing control, the
suspension soaking up the
bumps with an absorbent
100mm of travel not counting
the marshmallow tyres. It had
a further advantage over
conventional heavy 4x4s in not

compacting soil, and it rarely
left ruts.

Three-wheeler All-Terrain
Cycles (ATCs) were
introduced as the US90
in February 1970 and four-
wheeler ATV 250Rs, 200Xs,
and 125Ms in 1985.
Transmission by centrifugal
clutch, steering by handlebars,
and gearchanging by pedal –
with an extra-low ratio for
climbing – a child could drive it
if allowed. At their best when
invited to achieve the
seemingly impossible, such as
negotiating slopes (upwards or
downwards) unsuitable for
walking on, ATVs were
beautifully detailed. They had
indispensable gadgets such
as a headlamp on a 6ft cable,
useful for counting the bag
after a day on the grouse
moor, or (for aliens) finding
the way back to the flying
saucer at night.

In 1995 the Foreman with
a new air and oil-cooled
longitudinal engine improved
low-speed pulling power
to stay ahead of the
competition. ATVs had engines
from 86cc to 395cc, two wheel
drive or four wheel drive. By
the middle of the 1990s some
of Soichiro Honda's 1960s
predictions on air and oil
cooling were being borne out.

For Honda it was back to cars and motorcycles and generators and lawn mowers and cultivators and tractors. In 1991 the company was divided into separate divisions dealing with cars, motorcycles, and power products, each virtually autonomous and reflecting the changes of emphasis within Honda Motor. Motorcycle sales world-wide fell over a period of two decades and were no longer Honda's main source of income. By the 1990s they contributed only 10 per cent of Honda's entire sales and 1 per cent of its profits, cars were 70 per cent, other engines made up the rest. The research and development department was likewise divided up.

Yet motorcycling inventiveness was by no means exhausted and among the two-wheeled initiatives for the 1990s was a novel scooter, the CN250 which promised to be a Gold Wing sort of scooter, well-balanced, luxurious, and — for a scooter — large. The CN250 had a 64in wheelbase, a low centre of gravity, automatic transmission with smooth-running belt-and-pulleys, a quiet 250cc single cylinder water-cooled engine, and a fairing with a low windscreen to keep the weather off the rider. Honda's real scooter was the Bali, also with a continuously variable transmission (CVT) and a 49cc air-cooled two-stroke engine whose 5.5bhp provided a top speed of 30mph and a fuel consumption of 80mpg. There was no turpentine now, but in many ways it was not unlike the primitive little generator-engined bicycles with which the Honda story began. It provided marginal motoring for short, essential journeys, showing that for all its multinational airs and graces, its hard-won world championships on two wheels and four, and impeccable claims to be one of Paul Frère's "noble" makes, Honda never forgot where its roots lay. The Bali was not cheap, its customers were not on the breadline in a war-torn country, but it did the same kind of job, providing indispensable mobility to ordinary people.

In Britain the motorcycle market showed a recovery in the 1990s, with sales 10 per cent up and Honda enjoying a disproportionately large share of the improvement. The top six

Smart scooter of the 1990s, the Bali (left)

GOLD WING

A resplendent technological adventure, the 1975 flat-four GL1000 was derided at first as a curious two-wheeled car. The Gold Wing did not quite know what it was until the engine was made really big and it gained voluptuous fairings to constitute the most grandiloquent grand touring motorcycle ever.

probably more appropriate for serious touring. They said you could tell what sort of motorcycle it was simply by looking at the riders who effected dark glasses and Los Angeles Police Department-style headgear.

A flat-four engine, liquid cooling, shaft drive, generous dimensions, and a reputation for owners who never covered

too long. Under Toshio Nozue, the first production machine was the 999cc KO, large, heavy, and controversial. There was criticism of its handling – it was the first motorcycle that understeered like a nose-heavy car – but at 70mph it loped along at a mere 4,000rpm in contrast to its high-revving kin. A kickstart was available but it was stored in the toolbox

Quiet, smooth, and festooned with luxury equipment down to cruise control and an on-board compressor to inflate tyres or airbeds, it eventually gained the extra pair of cylinders to become a 1,520cc six. It could even be equipped with two extra wheels at the back to prevent it falling over at low speeds or when stationary.

With panniers, top-box, cruise control and reverse gear, and the rider – some would say driver – sitting comfortably on a sumptuous seat, it looked like the last word in intercontinental two-wheeled travel. By the 1990s the Gold Wing was a cult machine that its critics complained was suitable only for promenaders – the Pan-European V-4 was

large mileages, all conspired to make the Gold Wing, if not unique in motorcycling, at least a phenomenon to match the neo-vintage Harley-Davidson at one end of the spectrum and the marvellously high-tech BMWs at the other.

Soichiro Irimajiri's first thought for its engine in 1972 was the AOK, a six-cylinder of 1,470cc but it was simply

for emergencies.

The market, especially in America where the machine was aimed, was indifferent at first, but Honda was unperturbed. In 1980 it improved the ride and handling and began building it in the United States under Shuji Tanaka. With the Interstate and Aspencade models, it never looked back.

best-selling bikes were all Hondas led by the supersports CBR900RR Fireblade which upset the ordinary course of events by becoming Britain's best selling powered two-wheeler ahead of the Honda C90 step-thru. Third best-seller was the CBR600F, leading the 750cc sector. Fourth and fifth in the sales league were the most popular mopeds, the SH50 City Express and the Honda Vision, and sixth the 1994 CB500 twin.

Honda's return to a basics drawing board also produced the CBR600F and CBR1000F in 1987 so that, although the early 1980s may have represented something of a trough, by the 1990s recovery was complete with rational marketing, superb technical merit, and such innovations as single-arm rear suspension. Marketing initiatives included a two-year warranty, and the CBR600F was the UK's best selling 600cc bike for seven years out of eight.

Honda went to the top of all six sectors of the two-wheel market. These were mopeds; 100cc motorcycles; 125cc; 500cc; 750cc; and over 750cc motorcycles.

Its domination of the moped market sometimes meant it had more than 50 per cent of total sales, but the struggle for other sectors involved strenuous selling which brought innovations for the British motorcycle trade. Motorcycle dealers tended to be motorcycle enthusiasts, unlike more commercially minded car dealers who were in it for the money. Modern expensive motorcycles demanded modern expensive facilities and by the 1980s these sometimes outstripped the proficiency of motorcycle dealerships. Honda UK led the way in bringing the trade up to the mark when David Hancock, manager of sales and marketing, put up a three-year plan at the 1990 dealer conference in the Metropole Hotel, Birmingham, committing dealers to levels of stock and spares and standards of servicing, workshops and showrooms uncommon outside the largest dealerships. Showroom standards in particular were neglected and run down. "Some dealers didn't even switch the showroom lights on," said Hancock. A retail operations manual was set out, and 10 design centres for model showrooms established to demonstrate the way forward. Within 12 months rivals were following Honda's example.

Reflecting on Honda records on the Isle of Man, the Marysville-made Civic Coupe at Douglas (left)

Swindon Civic 5-door VTEC (below)

CIVIC

In the 1980s Honda in Britain had to deal with what, in marketing jargon, was an image problem. Curiously for a firm identified with powerful motorcycles, grand prix racing and memorable sports cars, the British thought of Hondas more as souls of reliability than transports of delight. The **CRX** and the **NSX** helped to change things, but the Civic Coupe of 1994 exemplified a new era.

The middle-aged had been fastidious customers. Prudent rather than parsimonious, they counted confidence more important than speed, style, comfort, or even safety. Encouraged by surveys that established Honda's credentials for reliability with only four faults per 100 vehicles – compared with Rover's (average) 40 and Renault's worst-case 98 – they could not get enough Civics. Following the trend towards down-sizing in the 1990s, the Civic Coupe was the right car at the right time and Honda UK began to import them from the United States.

It was cheap, cheerful, nimble, economical, well-proportioned, and it handled beautifully. Honda quickly doubled its estimate of how many it might sell and among the options were leather upholstery, air conditioning, alloy wheels, and sports suspension. Based on the Civic saloon but two inches longer than the hatchback in wheelbase and a foot longer overall, the Coupe had useful legroom in the back and headroom for average adults. Furthermore, it was not subject to the quota restrictions which inhibited imports from Japan.

Civic was as firmly established in the lexicon of motoring as Escort or Astra, yet until the 1990s it was something of a supermini with aspirations more Ford Fiesta than Ford Escort. It left the middle ground to the Honda Concerto and its Rover equivalent the 200-series until the beginning of production at Swindon brought change.

Plans for a new Civic, the sixth since the name was introduced in 1972, were laid before **BMW** bought Rover, but the upheaval made Honda stand up for itself, and the five-door Civic made at Swindon alongside the Accord was the first of a new breed.

Forbidding
clouds. Project
EXP-2, 1995
Granada-Dakar
Rally (below)

The aim was to tempt sophisticated 35-year-olds accustomed to being welcomed into car showrooms and greeted in a manner befitting people willing to spend several thousand important and hard-earned pounds. Honda UK reduced its stock from 16-17,000 bikes to around 2,000, ordering became more planned and better organised with 175 "A" dealers taking the full range of bikes and 99 "B" dealers going up to 500cc and obtaining bigger machines from the A-dealers. The results were swift to come through, with one 11-branch dealer reaching an annual turnover of £21 million.

By the 1990s Honda was looking for ways to introduce what it called "socially acceptable" motorcycles appealing beyond the dwindling numbers of traditional bikers to the big-spending leisure riders. The process began in America with the Gold Wing and then the Pacific Coast, a middleweight tourer with so much plastic cladding that it looked like a small two-wheeled car with a luggage boot.

The European equivalent was the ST (Sports Tourer) 1100 Pan-European, more recognisably a motorcycle but still intended to appear unaggressive and quiet. It was designed to comply with the reduction in noise levels planned for Europe and, be a

although by no means cheap and directed at BMW's executive market, it showed that Honda was still capable of tackling attractive niches. It had shaft drive and a 1,084cc, 100bhp V-4 engine with good pulling power that could cruise in top gear all day.

In 1995 Honda UK won a £1 million contract to supply the British Ministry of Defence with 104 ST1100P police motorcycles to replace BMWs and rotary-engined Nortons for the armed forces. It was a popular model with police, and 29 of Britain's 55 forces had ST1100Ps, as did the Automobile Association and the London Ambulance Service. The MoD's bikes were for escort duties and the military police.

Kawamoto's vision of Honda's future as a multinational corporation was clear when he spoke to the journalist Ray Hutton at the Tokyo Motor Show in 1993. He felt sure there would continue to be different ways of doing things at Honda subsidiaries in Japan, Europe and the US. He also saw strong progress in a fourth area, the developing countries where Honda had a manufacturing or sales activity.

American Honda Accords had a local content level of 82 per cent, and some cars such as the Civic Coupe and Accord Estate were American engineered and developed, yet it would

JOEY DUNLOP

One of the most popular of riders, small, untidy, an Irishman from Ballymoney, Co Antrim, Joey Dunlop eclipsed the opposition on four-stroke Honda V-4s in 1980s Formula One racing.

Almost unbeatable on the Isle of Man road course, where he most loved to race, he began riding for Honda in 1982 following a win with Yamaha in the 1978 Senior TT, and won the first of his five consecutive Formula One world titles. He took the record for the most TT wins.

be a long time before new models could be expected to be completely designed and built outside Japan. Engine development in particular would remain in Japan for a further 10 years even though it would be cheaper to follow Honda's well-known policy of giving local plants design autonomy wherever possible.

Rationalising worldwide strategy up to the year 2000 included planning fewer floorpans. Premium-priced cars would, by and large, have longitudinal engines while the Accord, Civic and minicar classes would be transverse-engined. Honda intended to carry on making microcars and Multi-Purpose Vehicles (MPVs) in response to demand for cheap, small minimum-specification cars from many Asian countries including the Philippines, Indonesia, Thailand, and Malaysia. Some of these markets remained satisfied with trucks, others moved to passenger cars of a size suitable for city traffic, something between a Honda Today and a Civic. Kawamoto wanted to meet the demand for a basic world car.

Honda moved into the MPV sector in 1994 with the Odyssey, introduced in Japan and shown at the Geneva motor show in 1995. A one-box six-seater based on the Accord with a 2.2-litre engine, it was the first MPV with a rear seat which retracted into the floor. It went on sale in the UK as the Honda Shuttle.

Although it never made its own leisure off-road 4x4, the market for them in Japan was too big for Honda to ignore. It introduced the Land Rover Discovery as the Honda Crossroad, the first foreign vehicle sold in Japan to bear the name of a domestic manufacturer. Honda also sold its own version of the Isuzu Trooper but never produced it itself. "We had the old Civic Shuttle 4x4; it didn't sell very well. Perhaps it was a little early for the market," said Kawamoto. The Civic's 4x4 system would have made a rugged sports/utility with an alternative body but although Honda studied the idea it never put it into effect.

"They are not often used off-road, even in the United States," said Kawamoto. "They carry around such big tyres and diesel engines and heavy transmissions and drive systems that cost a great deal and seldom get used. That seems a waste of money. We have saved the investment for making a chassis or big diesel engines or military-class drive systems. Range Rover is already a big name Japan. It is the brand leader."

Honda never made a diesel car, and for markets which demanded diesel cars it bought in engines. "We like diesel engines but we have been unable to find a way of resolving the emission control problems, notably NO^x. Reducing NO^x is a big obstacle in Japan where the transport authorities want diesels to meet the same target for emissions as small petrol trucks and passenger cars. We have studied an NO^x reduction catalyst for lean-burn engines and if we can make it, we could use it on petrol and diesel. It is one of the more challenging projects we are carrying out, and we are also looking at a particulate trap."

HONDA NSX

The first modern production car made almost entirely in aluminium, the **NSX** – New Sports eXperimental – of 1991 brought Honda into the cherished company of automotive classics such as Ferrari and Porsche. Honda, in Paul Frère's words "ennobled" itself through motor racing; now it demanded entry into the club of classic road cars. Yet with the **NSX** it contested the ideology of the sports car. It showed that fast cars need not be quirky or difficult or demanding to drive. The **NSX** was quiet, refined, smooth, and comfortable.

Mid-engined, beautifully proportioned, exquisitely hand-made in its own small factory at Tochigii, and for a car competing in such a specialised market quite reasonably priced, the **NSX** was well received from the start. It was every bit as fast as its principal rivals, probably faster on the road on account of its superior ride and precise handling. Some of the first cars that reached the UK were advertised at a handsome premium. Only 25 of the 3ft 10in tall mid-engined coupes were made every day, which made them as exclusive as any Ferrari and rarer than a Porsche.

The **NSX** had the elegance of both without the highly-strung nature of either. Unlike many Ferraris, it never demanded great deftness at the wheel, although with 274bhp available from the

3-litre **V-6** engine it demanded concentration. Honda drew on its racing experience for some of the radical features such as the lightweight (and expensive) titanium connecting rods. Even the exemplary racing car-style suspension was aluminium. It reached 60mph in less than 5.0sec and had a top speed of 167mph.

Thirty years before the **NSX**, the E-Type Jaguar showed that racing-car handling was not incompatible with smoothness and refinement. Drivers who pined for stiff springing and a noisy engine in 1961, were as out of tune with the times as their successors who disparaged the **NSX** for lacking character or failing some quaint test of machismo.

The **NSX** was safe because it would never betray a semi-skilled driver, yet its fine poise and good balance provided ample reward for the proficient. It inspired confidence as the mid-engined layout put the bulk of the weight in the middle where it made neither the front nor the back swing wide. The balance was perfect, provoking no tail slides, no front-wheel skids, and the ride was as supple as a small saloon.

The powerful brakes produced a stopping power of over 1g, with the fat, specially developed Yokohama tyres gripping the road with great might. It was as tolerant in the wet as in the dry.

The interior was scarcely

grand, with a plain, clear instrument display, and agreeable stitched leather seats. A basin-shaped bin behind the high-revving masterpiece of an engine served as a luggage boot. The **NSX** could crawl along in traffic making no more noise than an Accord, then accelerate to nearly 170mph, doing over 8,000rpm in the gears and sounding like a thoroughbred.

Previewed at the 1995 Detroit motor show, an open-topped version had technical innovations which included F-Matic, a new semi-automatic transmission controlled from buttons on the steering wheel like a Formula One car. It did away with the mechanical linkage between the accelerator pedal and the engine; the throttle worked by a progressive electric switch, improving management of the TCS (Traction Control System) limiting wheelspin.

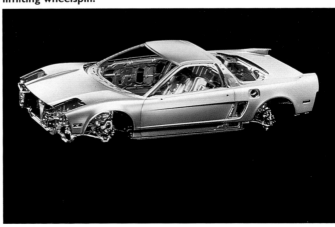

Exquisite form, impeccable pedigree (left)

High-tech VTEC. The NSX V-6 engine (below left)

Triumph of technology. The hand-made aluminium framework of NSX (below)

Casino square, 1989. Legend Coupe (right)

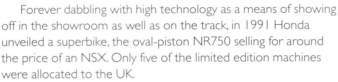

In effect a V-8 of watch-making precision (left)

Four into two will go. Four-by-four-valve heads (far left)

Two connecting rods, one elliptical piston with clearances for eight valves (below left)

Forever dabbling with high technology as a means of showing off in the showroom as well as on the track, in 1991 Honda unveiled a superbike, the oval-piston NR750 selling for around the price of an NSX. Only five of the limited edition machines were allocated to the UK.

Oval pistons seemed an unlikely novelty when they were introduced for the NR500 racer of 1977. They were a "... historical accident," according the journalist L J K Setright, "the product of racing rules which distort natural engineering development by setting artificial limits to the number of cylinders an engine might have."

Honda found in the 1970s that its traditional four-strokes stood little chance against the two-strokes dominating motorcycle racing, but with its aptitude for original concepts it reflected that pistons do not necessarily have to be round. Faced with a 36mm stroke to achieve suitable volumetric efficiency, and allowed only four cylinders by the regulations, Honda engineers hit on the idea of oval cylinders which gave room in the cylinder head for two combustion chambers per cylinder. This provided eight in all, so although there were only four cylinders and four pistons, the engine was effectively a small V-8.

The V-4 oval-piston road-going NR750 had two titanium connecting-rods, and a similar cylinder head with twice as many combustion chambers, spark plugs, valves and fuel injectors as any other V-4. Power output was 125bhp at 14,000rpm. The wheels were magnesium, the bodywork carbon-fibre, the space frame aluminium. It had single swing-arm rear suspension and inverted front forks that came straight from the Honda endurance racers.

Four-valve
Fantasy...
(below)

The aluminium construction of the NSX was reflected in the FSX concept luxury car which had such lightweight construction it needed only a 3.5-litre V-6 VTEC engine to provide the speed and acceleration the luxury market expected. Inside, it had a cellular telephone and a television screen for back seat occupants. The driver was provided with a TV monitor covering all angles close to the car which could not be seen from the driving seat. Its colour liquid crystal display (LCD) doubled up as an on-board navigation system.

Honda went a long way in Britain. In thirty years it grew from being a low-key importer of motorcycles and power equipment to a major producer of cars for Britain and Europe. Honda's inward investment which started with £370 million went up by a further £240 million to add other products to the Accord and Civic 5-door models made at South Marston, putting Honda on track to sell 300,000 cars in Europe by the end of the century.

Yet even in an age of electronics and multi-national global business complexity Honda's heart remained in engines. Their distinctive appearance gave them the character of modern sculptures, the silvery sheen of Honda die-castings and the elegant cooling fins had a whiff of Oriental artistry. Honda never was double-barrelled, only multi-cylindered.

BIBLIOGRAPHY

Honda, ed Mick Woollett; Temple Press, 1983
Honda, Roy Bacon; Sunburst Books, 1995
Honda, The Man and his Machines, Sol Sanders; Tuttle, 1975
Honda, The Complete Story, Roland Brown; Crowood 1991
Honda, Mick Walker; Osprey 1993
The NSX, Bulgin, McGrandle, Setright, Tremayne, Ward; Redwood
Honda Motor, Tetsuo Sakiya; Kodansha 1982
Honda France, 25 Ans Déja; EPA 1989
Honda Gold Wing, Malcolm Birkitt; Osprey 1995
A Decade of Continuous Challenges; Honda Motor Co Ltd

Honda Owners Club
Chairman Norman Hacker, 35 Fanshawe Crescent, Ware, Herts SG12
0AR. Club magazine *'Revs!'*

Membership and S800 Register
Christopher Wallwork, 23A High Street, Steeton, Keighley, West Yorks,
BD20 6NT

N and Z Register
Simon Hume, 14 The Knapps Semington, Trowbridge, Wiltshire BA19
6JG. John Russell, 59 Fulton Avenue, West Kirby, Merseyside, L48 6EY.
Gary Hargreaves, Flat 2D, Ridge Road, Crouch End, London N8 9LG

Honda Driver's Club
51 Conway Road, Colwyn Bay, LL29 7AW. Club magazine *'Pride'*

ACKNOWLEDGMENTS

The author and publisher would like to thank Toshio Ishino, managing director Honda UK, Paul Ormond, Caroline Horsman, Ian Shaw, Laurence Pearce and Graham Sanderson of the Honda UK press department, Anne Bridges of Honda Power equipment, and Ken Keir director and general manager, car division for their help and encouragement in publishing this book.

Our thanks go to Barry Bolton for editing the manuscript, and our secretary Diane Lappage for her notable contribution to its production including researching our own photographic archives.

Peter Burn carried out the specially commissioned photography, and Japanese background and picture research was accomplished by Japan Archives of Leeds. Our thanks go also to Phil Masters, David Phipps of Phipps Photographic, LAT Photographic and the National Motor Museum Picture Library at Beaulieu. McLaren International and Williams Grand Prix Engineering allowed Peter Burn to photograph their historic racing car collections.

We owe special thanks to Michael Turner for permission to use his painting of Richie Ginther's Honda at Silverstone, and Craig Warwick and David and Chris Mills of Grand Prix Sportique of Tetbury for allowing us to reproduce their print of Ayrton Senna. Marlboro authorised the use of racing photographs from Jad Sherif of Geneva, and EMAP of Peterborough supplied the historic TT photograph of racing at Ginger Hall. Thanks are due to Ray Hutton for making available his extensive interviews with Nobuhiko Kawamoto.

Honda S800 owners Norman Hacker and John Howie willingly turned out their splendid cars for photography, and Mick Woollett kindly looked into his photo archives for pictures of early Hondas.

INDEX